I0605949

TO:
FROM:
DATE:

STRENGTH
for the
STRUGGLES

MARILEE PARRISH

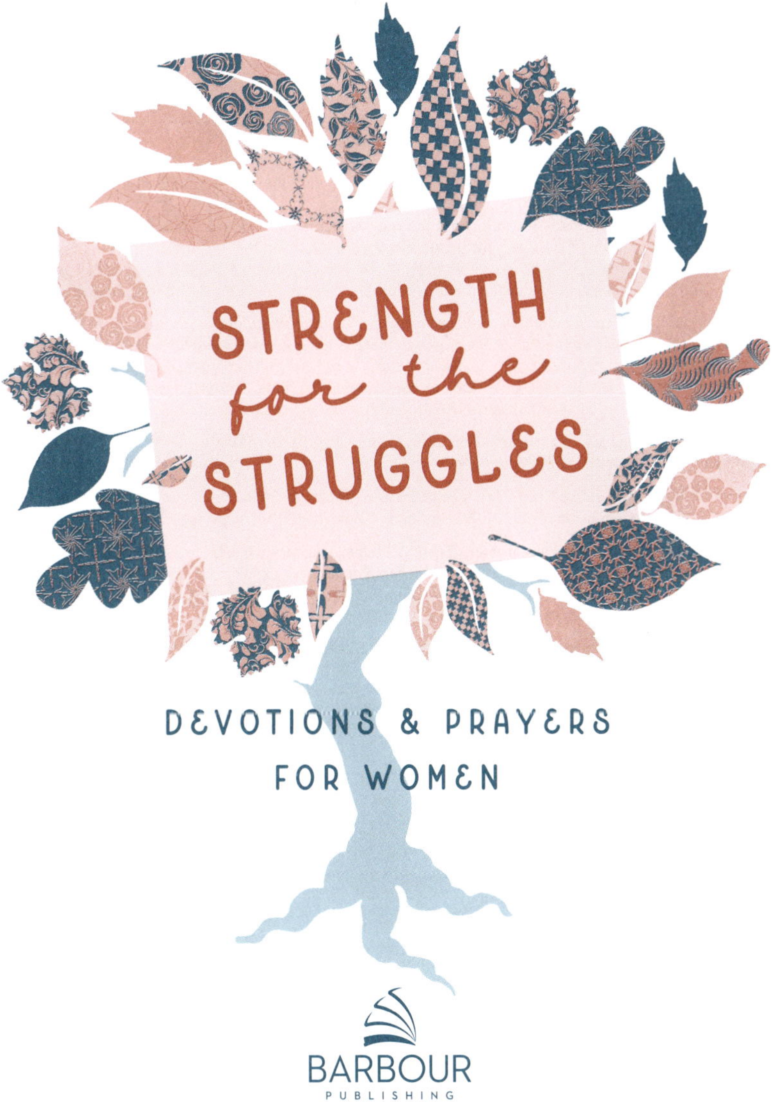

STRENGTH for the STRUGGLES

DEVOTIONS & PRAYERS FOR WOMEN

YOU are the reason we do what we do here at Barbour Publishing. We promise that we will always use our God-given talents to produce content with you in mind—and that we will remain biblically faithful, no matter what.

Thank you for being the heart of our business.

Print ISBN 979-8-89151-253-5

Cover design by Greg Jackson, Thinkpen Design

Published by Barbour Publishing, Inc., 1810 Barbour Drive, Uhrichsville, Ohio 44683, www.barbourbooks.com

Our mission is to inspire the world with the life-changing message of the Bible.

Printed in China.

INTRODUCTION

"There is no 'You've got this,'" my wise friend Linette wrote to me in a text.

Hmm. I hadn't heard that before! What was she getting at?

When we're struggling, it's easy to try and talk ourselves into action. Have you ever said any of these phrases to yourself while looking in the mirror?

"You've got this!"

"You are enough!"

"You're never given more than you can handle."

We hear these messages from the self-help world a lot, and sometimes even well-meaning Christians pass these words along to us. But if we're being honest, there are times when "You've got this" just isn't true. Sometimes we *aren't* enough. Sometimes the situations we're in are way more than we can handle on our own. And it's in our words of surrender that we find the one who is enough—*Jesus*!

My friend Linette meant that only Jesus could be the strength I needed in the overwhelming situation I was in. Jesus Himself. Not my strength, but *His*.

Philippians 2:13 (AMPC) says, "[Not in your own strength] for it is God Who is all the while effectually at work in you [energizing and creating in you the power and desire], both to will and to work for His good pleasure and satisfaction and delight."

Let's unpack these powerful words together as we spend time in these devotions!

With you on the journey,
MariLee

WHEN YOU JUST CAN'T

I want to know Christ and experience the mighty power that raised him from the dead.

PHILIPPIANS 3:10 NLT

Financial troubles. Health problems. Relationship issues. Work difficulties. Every day seems to overflow with struggles. Sometimes it seems like you can't take one more thing. Does God see? Is He even there? Doubts creep in, and you feel alone in your struggles. How will you get through one more day of this?

It's tempting to scroll through your phone for hours on end to get your mind off things. Resist that, friend! Instead, let these words guide you:

- "The LORD will fight for you; you need only to be still" (Exodus 14:14 NIV).
- "Be still, and know that I am God" (Psalm 46:10 ESV).

Right now, take a few minutes to be still. Close your eyes. Ask Jesus to quiet your mind. Picture yourself boldly approaching His throne of grace (Hebrews 4:16). Let His grace wash over you. Let His love invade your heart. Stay in that safe place where nothing else matters but Jesus. Don't think about your problems. Just seek His face. Chase after His presence. There's definitely something to that old hymn that promises, "The things of earth will grow strangely dim in the light of His glory and grace."

JESUS, SHOW ME WHAT IT MEANS TO BE STILL BEFORE YOU AND TO KNOW THAT YOU ARE GOD.

APPROACH HIS THRONE DAILY

But he said to me, "My grace is sufficient for you, for my power is made perfect in weakness." Therefore I will boast all the more gladly about my weaknesses, so that Christ's power may rest on me. That is why, for Christ's sake, I delight in weaknesses, in insults, in hardships, in persecutions, in difficulties. For when I am weak, then I am strong.

2 CORINTHIANS 12:9–10 NIV

The best—and only—way to get through life's struggles with your heart intact is this: "Let us then approach God's throne of grace with confidence, so that we may receive mercy and find grace to help us in our time of need" (Hebrews 4:16 NIV).

Spending time in the heavenly Father's presence needs to be a daily thing. Sometimes it needs to be a moment-by-moment thing. Practice going to His throne and letting Him love you. Start your day by being still before Him. Whisper His name as you brew your coffee or pack your lunch. Picture His grace washing over you, filling you with His strength.

The distraction of busyness will always threaten to take over your thoughts. But if you practice being still before God, even for just a few minutes at a time, you will always find supernatural strength available to you (Ephesians 1:19)!

LORD, I BELIEVE YOUR GRACE IS ENOUGH FOR ME.

PLUGGING INTO THE SOURCE

I also pray that you will understand the incredible greatness of God's power for us who believe him. This is the same mighty power that raised Christ from the dead and seated him in the place of honor at God's right hand in the heavenly realms.

EPHESIANS 1:19–20 NLT

Imagine a window air-conditioning unit capable of cooling down a stifling room on a hot summer day. But someone forgot to plug it in! So the room remains uncomfortable and nearly uninhabitable while the source of cool air sits there accessible but unused.

The Bible tells us that God's power for us as believers is the same power that raised Christ from the dead! *The Message* says, "Oh, the utter extravagance of his work in us who trust him—endless energy, boundless strength!" (Ephesians 1:19).

Endless energy? Boundless strength? Wow! How does *that* happen? How can I get those things? Just like that air-conditioning unit that remains unplugged, we can't access God's power without first connecting to the power source.

Jeremiah 29:13 (NIV) says, "You will seek me and find me when you seek me with all your heart."

Practice being still before God. Seek His face. Get into His Word.

LORD JESUS, OPEN MY EYES SO I CAN UNDERSTAND WHAT YOU'RE SAYING TO ME. HELP ME BELIEVE THAT YOU WANT TO FILL ME WITH YOUR STRENGTH. SHOW ME HOW I CAN GET PLUGGED IN TO YOU.

EMPOWERED TO SURRENDER

I can do everything through Christ, who gives me strength.
PHILIPPIANS 4:13 NLT

Today's verse is one that is often committed to memory. Athletes wear it on T-shirts. Students claim it as their favorite scripture. Christians encountering a difficult task can be heard whispering it through gritted teeth. But what does it mean, and how can a person tap into Christ's strength?

Check out Philippians 4:13 in the Amplified Bible: "I can do all things [which He has called me to do] through Him who strengthens and empowers me [to fulfill His purpose—I am self-sufficient in Christ's sufficiency; I am ready for anything and equal to anything through Him who infuses me with inner strength and confident peace.]"

That sheds some more light on the meaning, doesn't it? We can do *all* the things that God calls us to, not just random things that we decide to do on our own. Christ is the one doing the strengthening and empowering. He is the one filling us with inner strength. This is not a "grit our teeth and power through" verse. It is a surrendering of our strength for His as He fulfills His purposes in and through us.

LORD, I CAN'T HANDLE ALL MY RESPONSIBILITIES ON MY OWN. I DON'T HAVE THE STRENGTH. I'M READY TO SURRENDER TO YOUR WILL AND YOUR WAYS IN MY LIFE.

GRIPPED BY FAITH, NOT BY FEAR

All those prayers are coming together now so you will do this well, fearless in your struggle, keeping a firm grip on your faith and on yourself.

1 TIMOTHY 1:18–19 MSG

When you're in the middle of a struggle, it's more than likely that fear is right there, your constant companion. Fear likes to creep in and grab hold of anyone who opens the door to it.

It seems unlikely, but is it possible to be fearless in your struggles?

One Christian speaker shared that he grew up with an extremely controlling mother. This caused him to be very passive, which eventually caused problems in his marriage. A young mother who heard his story let fear grip her heart. She was afraid that some of her own control issues would be passed on to her child in negative ways, just like the speaker had experienced.

But the Holy Spirit reminded her that the sins of parents don't have to be passed to their children anymore. . .because of Jesus! Instead of letting fear take root, she sat in God's presence and allowed His perfect love to cast out the fear she had been feeling (1 John 4:18).

This, friend, is how to become fearless in any struggle! Hold tightly to Christ's perfect love, and fear won't stand a chance.

LORD JESUS, AS I DWELL IN YOUR HOLY PRESENCE, LET YOUR PERFECT LOVE CAST OUT EVERY FEAR.

EVER-PRESENT HELP

God is our refuge and strength, an ever-present help in trouble.

Psalm 46:1 niv

In this mixed-up world, trouble will come to us from time to time. Jesus told us to be prepared but also to "take heart" (John 16:33 niv) and to trust Him.

The Amplified Bible, Classic Edition, explains Psalm 46:1 this way: "God is our Refuge and Strength [mighty and impenetrable to temptation], a very present and well-proved help in trouble."

In Christ we find a strength that is mighty! It's a supernatural strength that's "impenetrable to temptation." Wow! How many of us need to be rescued from the trouble we find ourselves in when we cave to temptation? Imagine a strength that temptation can't penetrate! *That's* what you'll find in Christ! If you learn to abide in Him (John 15) and allow His Spirit to fill you, His strength will become yours.

God is ever present. He's always available to you, no appointment needed. He wants to help you through all your struggles. He is also your refuge, a safe place to run when you're in trouble. You'll find His arms wide open at all times.

His strength is perfect. You're going to need it!

LORD, THANK YOU FOR BEING MY EVER-PRESENT HELP. YOUR STRENGTH IS PERFECT. FILL ME WITH YOUR SPIRIT AS I SEEK YOU.

THE WILSONS' STORY, PART 1

Jesus looked at [his disciples] intently and said, "Humanly speaking, it is impossible. But with God everything is possible."

MATTHEW 19:26 NLT

Every mom's worst nightmare happened two weeks before Christmas. A call came in from Tiffani's daughter, Arwen, that she'd been in a terrible car accident with her younger brothers. They were all bumped and bruised, but Tiffani's twelve-year-old son was unconscious and bleeding. He was taken to the nearest trauma center.

Our dear friends Tiffani and Aaron rushed to the scene of the accident. They were not able to ride with their son to the emergency room. When they were finally together at the hospital with their wounded child, they were not given much hope. It looked like their son Jackson wasn't going to make it.

Tiffani desperately needed to hear from God. She turned to God's Word as her family faced the darkest struggle of their lives. What she found astonished her. You'll hear more about this in part 2 on the next page. This true story of how God gave a family strength during a horrific tragedy is proof that God is alive and at work in our lives in miraculous ways.

LORD, I BELIEVE THAT YOU ARE THE SAME GOD OF MIRACLES YOU'VE ALWAYS BEEN. THANK YOU FOR SHOWING UP IN POWERFUL WAYS IN OUR LIVES TODAY!

THE WILSONS' STORY, PART 2

Indeed, we felt we had received the sentence of death. But this happened that we might not rely on ourselves but on God, who raises the dead.

2 CORINTHIANS 1:9 NIV

The emergency department at the nearest hospital worked to get Jackson stable enough to be life-flighted to the children's hospital. The winds that night were very high, and Tiffani and Aaron were not permitted to ride along.

Tiffani turned to God and His Word. Second Corinthians 1 popped out at her. It was precisely what God wanted her to know in that moment. She was encouraged by The Passion Translation, which words it this way: "All of the hardships we passed through crushed us beyond our ability to endure, and we were so completely overwhelmed that we were about to give up entirely. It felt like we had a death sentence written upon our hearts. . . . It has taught us to lose all faith in ourselves and to place all of our trust in the God who raises the dead. . . . And now we fasten our hopes on him to continue to deliver us from death yet again" (verses 8–10).

This was the hope Tiffani clung to for dear life—hers and her son's. (You'll learn more in the next devotional reading.)

YOU ARE CLOSER THAN WE UNDERSTAND, JESUS. THANK YOU FOR SPEAKING TO US SO CLEARLY THROUGH YOUR WORD!

PRAYERS FOR JACKSON

On [God] we have set our hope that he will continue to deliver us, as you help us by your prayers. Then many will give thanks on our behalf for the gracious favor granted us in answer to the prayers of many.

2 CORINTHIANS 1:10–11 NIV

Phones lit up all over Northern Indiana and beyond, sharing the message that the Wilsons needed fervent prayers for Jackson's life. Friends and loved ones got on their knees. A prayer chain in Colorado heard about the need. A group of young teens sat in a circle at a tournament, praying for a boy they didn't know in Indiana. An elderly woman in Ohio who had been far from God her entire life heard about Jackson, and his situation tugged on her heartstrings. She began praying too.

God was at work.

These words from 2 Corinthians kept the Wilson family going, especially after a difficult night of unstable vitals for Jackson and a time of complete surrender for Tiffani and her husband: "Because there are so many interceding for us, our deliverance will cause even more people to give thanks to God. What a gracious gift of mercy surrounds us because of your prayers!" (1:11 TPT).

LORD, YOUR WORD TELLS ME THAT OUR PRAYERS ARE POWERFUL AND EFFECTIVE (JAMES 5:16). I MAY NOT FULLY UNDERSTAND IT, BUT I PUT ALL MY HOPE AND TRUST IN YOU!

JACKSON'S MIRACLE

You are the God who performs miracles;
you display your power among the peoples.
PSALM 77:14 NIV

Around midnight it was determined that Jackson needed brain surgery. His parents were still driving to the hospital at that time. A titanium plate and screws were put in. Doctors wouldn't know the extent of brain damage until more CT scans were taken. Tiffani's boy was unconscious for more than a week.

The family soon learned that the brain surgery was successful, and Jackson began to improve daily—against all odds. However, there were many nights when his vitals were again unstable, and his situation began to look grim. But prayers all over the United States continued. Jackson was a fighter, and God was at work sustaining and healing him.

After fourteen days in the ICU, Jackson was moved to a regular room for recovery. He graduated from intensive care on Christmas Day, and it was one of the best gifts the Wilson family could ever receive.

Still, they were told by a therapist that Jackson would likely need to relearn everything and start at the beginning in school. But two weeks later, Jackson was able to perform in a play and recited all the lines he had memorized *before* the accident!

WOW, GOD! YOU ARE AMAZING AND WONDERFUL!
THANK YOU FOR YOUR HEALING POWER!

BAD NEWS

They will have no fear of bad news; their hearts are steadfast, trusting in the LORD. Their hearts are secure, they will have no fear; in the end they will look in triumph on their foes.

PSALM 112:7–8 NIV

When you go through several struggles in a short period of time, you might start to feel paranoid, like the other shoe is always about to drop. Like joy will be stolen in an instant. Worry and fear lurk around every corner.

If you find yourself thinking these negative thoughts, it's time to give God authority over your thoughts. The enemy lies to you, but you don't have to agree or accept his lies! Second Corinthians 10:5 (NIV) says, "We demolish arguments and every pretension that sets itself up against the knowledge of God, and we take captive every thought to make it obedient to Christ."

When you are in a constant state of worry and you always fear bad news, you are picturing a future without Jesus. Instead, drown out those worrisome thoughts with the truth!

Your trust is in God. He loves you and has good plans for you. He will never leave you nor forsake you!

LORD, I REPENT OF FEARING BAD NEWS. I NO LONGER ALIGN MYSELF WITH LIES THE ENEMY TELLS ME. I WILL TELL MYSELF TRUTH FROM YOUR WORD AND TRUST YOU TO BE WITH ME ALWAYS.

DESPAIR OR REST?

Yet I am confident I will see the LORD's goodness
while I am here in the land of the living.
PSALM 27:13 NLT

The Amplified Bible says it this way: "I would have despaired had I not believed that I would see the goodness of the LORD in the land of the living."

Jesus said that He came to give us an abundant life (John 10:10). Getting buried by our struggles doesn't sound like a full and abundant life, does it? Yet, this is where we often find ourselves.

Having strength for the struggles sometimes looks like taking boundaries more seriously. It involves learning when to say no to good things and good people for your own mental health and the health of those you love most. Having good boundaries helps you make space for quiet time with Jesus—the place where you find strength for living. Then you have space to do those things that God is calling you specifically to do (remember Philippians 4:13 in the Amplified Bible)!

When despair is calling your name, remember that Jesus calls you to an abundant life in Him. He is calling you to come to Him and rest (Matthew 11:28–30).

JESUS, I NEED SPACE IN MY LIFE TO HEAR FROM YOU. FILL ME WITH YOUR GOODNESS AND PEACE. GIVE ME STRENGTH TO CREATE NECESSARY BOUNDARIES IN MY LIFE.

WHEN TROUBLE COMES

"I have told you these things, so that in me you may have peace. In this world you will have trouble. But take heart! I have overcome the world."

JOHN 16:33 NIV

Author and speaker John Eldredge says that worrying is a "violation of faith, hope, and love." Worrying is sinful. Jesus says not to do it! So what about scriptures like this one that tell us we're guaranteed to have trouble? Shouldn't we be ready for that? Bad things *will* happen!

Jesus promises us that if we remain in Him, we can have His peace no matter what happens! Instead of imagining what bad thing might happen next or all the horrible things that could be happening with a loved one who is late or not responding to your texts, you instead seek God's face. You get in His Word. You take your thoughts captive and wrap yourself in biblical truth.

Philippians 4:6–7 (NLT) says, "Don't worry about anything; instead, pray about everything. Tell God what you need, and thank him for all he has done. Then you will experience God's peace, which exceeds anything we can understand. His peace will guard your hearts and minds as you live in Christ Jesus."

LORD JESUS, I REPENT OF WORRYING! HELP ME COME TO YOU INSTEAD OF FEARING BAD NEWS AND SPECULATING ABOUT THE FUTURE.

GOD HEARS

As for me, I call to God, and the LORD saves me. Evening, morning and noon I cry out in distress, and he hears my voice. He rescues me unharmed from the battle waged against me, even though many oppose me.

PSALM 55:16–18 NIV

Worn out. Tired. Discouraged. Afraid. Have these words ever described you? Too much is on your plate, and you feel like you have to eat every crumb. Maybe you were raised to clean your plate and you've carried that into adulthood.

The Psalms are a great place to spend time when you are feeling overwhelmed. You will find honest, raw emotions. Sadness. Depression. Anger. Fear. But you'll also find hope and help. When you pour out your raw feelings to God, you'll find that He meets you where you are. He can handle your honesty. You don't have to clean up your thoughts before you take them to God. He will help you sort everything out.

If you find that you take your emotions and anger out on the people who live closest to you, it's a sure sign that you need some extended alone time with God. Go somewhere quiet and private and talk to Jesus. Write out your prayers beforehand if that's helpful to you.

LORD, I'M BRINGING ALL MY THOUGHTS AND FEELINGS TO YOU NOW. I TRUST THAT YOU SEE ME. HELP ME SORT THINGS OUT.

GOD'S HAND AT WORK

When anxiety was great within me,
your consolation brought me joy.
PSALM 94:19 NIV

The Message says it this way: "If GOD hadn't been there for me, I never would have made it. The minute I said, 'I'm slipping, I'm falling,' your love, GOD, took hold and held me fast. When I was upset and beside myself, you calmed me down and cheered me up" (verses 17–19).

Have you ever taken an inventory of your life? Have you looked back over the years and asked God to show you those times when His hand was at work? This exercise can bring a lot of peace, joy, and "aha!" moments. You don't need a lot of time to do this. You can start slow. Begin with elementary school and ask God to reveal where He had His hand on you. What He allowed or didn't in your life. Write down anything that comes to mind. Then, as you have time in the coming weeks, do this for each decade of your life.

The consolation of seeing God move at certain times in your life can be very powerful. When you've finished your inventory, share it with a trusted friend or family member.

LORD GOD, I'M SO THANKFUL FOR ALL THE WAYS YOU HAVE SHOWN UP IN MY LIFE! I'M AMAZED AT HOW YOU CARE FOR ME.

BROKEN BUT BEAUTIFUL

But we have this treasure in jars of clay to show that this all-surpassing power is from God and not from us. We are hard pressed on every side, but not crushed; perplexed, but not in despair; persecuted, but not abandoned; struck down, but not destroyed.

2 CORINTHIANS 4:7–9 NIV

Feeling bruised and broken? Our humanness keeps us humble and reminds us that our strength comes from God and not from us. You've probably felt hard pressed, perplexed, and struck down at different times in your life. But you will never be crushed, in despair, or destroyed. The truth is that even when we feel utterly defeated, there's always hope.

Though you may feel like a broken jar at times, Jesus Christ is alive and at work in you! He is actively putting the pieces of your life back together as you place them in His hands. He can take your brokenness and mold you into something beautiful.

Ephesians 3:16 (NLT) says, "I pray that from his glorious, unlimited resources he will empower you with inner strength through his Spirit."

Let that be your prayer today!

LORD, PLEASE EMPOWER ME WITH INNER STRENGTH THAT COMES SOLELY FROM YOU. LET YOUR SPIRIT COME ALIVE IN ME AND TRANSFORM MY BROKENNESS INTO SOMETHING BEAUTIFUL.

THE LORD IS MY STRENGTH

I was pushed back and about to fall, but the Lord helped me. The Lord is my strength and my defense; he has become my salvation.

Psalm 118:13–14 NIV

A woman's voice came over the Christian radio station. She was talking about holiness. She said that if we love God, we will choose holiness. When sin tempts us, we will simply turn the other way because we love God. The flaw in that thinking may be that we are turning away "in our own strength." And if we continue to turn from sin in our own strength, couldn't pride take over just like it did with the Pharisees?

What about those who struggle with addictions? If they could just turn from sin, they would do it! The strength they need to turn from sinful addictions has to come from a supernatural power outside of themselves. Strongholds need to be broken in the power and authority of Jesus Christ. They can't be taken down in one's own strength.

The key that the radio commentator was missing is that Jesus Christ Himself becomes our strength to turn from sin. He *is* our strength. When we can't, He can. Where we fail, He brings the victory.

JESUS, YOU ALONE ARE MY STRENGTH. YOUR POWER IS ALIVE AND AT WORK IN ME. THANK YOU.

LOOK TO THE LORD

Look to the Lord and his strength; seek his face always.

Psalm 105:4 NIV

First Thessalonians 5:16–18 (NIV) says, "Rejoice always, pray continually, give thanks in all circumstances; for this is God's will for you in Christ Jesus."

Be unceasing in prayer? How can I possibly seek His face always? I can't pray all day. I have a busy life!

When the Bible urges us to pray continually, it's not a suggestion that we abandon our lives and pray on our knees from sunup to sundown. But it is a daily heart posture. It is recognizing that God is alive and at work in us in every situation. It is acknowledging and honoring His presence that is available to us at every moment.

If you want strength to face whatever comes your way, start and end each day with prayer. When you wake up, thank God for another day to be a light for Him. Get in His Word before you begin your work so that you have the sword of the Spirit at the ready. Women are amazing multitaskers! When you find yourself in a difficult situation during your day, acknowledge God's presence and ask Him for help.

Look to the Lord throughout your day, and you will find that His strength will get you through anything!

THANK YOU FOR GIVING ME YOUR STRENGTH EACH DAY, LORD!

THE JOY OF THE LORD

"The joy of the Lord is your strength."
Nehemiah 8:10 NIV

"I've lost my joy!" A young mom cried to a Christian counselor after experiencing some devastating circumstances. She had been a joyful person most of her life. This feeling of depression was completely foreign to her.

We know that joy and happiness are not the same. Joy is a fruit of the Spirit (Galatians 5:22–23) that can only be found by remaining in the vine. John 15:5 (NIV) says, "I am the vine; you are the branches. If you remain in me and I in you, you will bear much fruit; apart from me you can do nothing."

By remaining in Christ—the vine—the fruit of the Spirit can grow in us. Love, joy, and peace begin to show up in our lives in tangible ways. This young mom had allowed circumstances and people to pull at her until she was left hanging to the vine by nothing more than a dried-up twig. We need wise Christians to come alongside us and lift us up from time to time.

The Christian counselor worked weekly with this young mother to help her find her joy again, reminding her that "the joy of the Lord" is where she could find the strength she needed to overcome her depression.

JESUS, THANK YOU FOR SENDING ALONG OTHER BELIEVERS WHO CAN HELP US FIND OUR WAY BACK TO JOY!

THE STRUGGLE IS REAL

The Lord is a refuge for the oppressed,
a stronghold in times of trouble.
Psalm 9:9 NIV

All throughout the Bible we can read true stories of God's people who found strength in Him in the middle of their struggles. Remembering these people when we're going through hard times can be very helpful. These stories aren't just Sunday School stories for children. They are about *real* people who depended on a *real* God to help them through their *real* problems.

Joseph was thrown into a pit by his brothers who lied and told their father he was dead. Leah was humiliated and unloved by her husband. Hannah wanted to be a mother and was mocked by her husband's second wife for being childless. Daniel was thrown into a den of lions. David was hunted by a king and had to run for his life. Ruth lost her husband and moved to a foreign country with her mother-in-law. Job lost everything. Elijah was depressed and wanted to die. Mary was a pregnant, unwed teenager. The apostle Paul was thrown into prison several times.

We're going to take a closer look at these stories on the next several pages. You'll see that God was their strength *then*, just as He is our strength *now*.

LORD, I'M SO THANKFUL FOR YOUR WORD THAT SPEAKS REAL-LIFE ENCOURAGEMENT INTO MY LIFE TODAY!

JOSEPH

But Joseph said to them, "Don't be afraid. Am I in the place of God? You intended to harm me, but God intended it for good to accomplish what is now being done, the saving of many lives. So then, don't be afraid. I will provide for you and your children." And he reassured them and spoke kindly to them.

GENESIS 50:19–21 NIV

Joseph had a lot of brothers—from the same dad but various mothers. Joseph knew he was his dad's favorite. His siblings grew abusive toward him because he was young and arrogant. It took many years and a lot of humility and growing up for this story to unfold. But miraculous reconciliation did eventually take place. (You can read the whole story in the book of Genesis to get all the details.)

If you're in the middle of a family or other relationship struggle, hold on to hope. You can't fix it, but God sure can. Don't rush Him. It took more than twenty years for Joseph to be reconciled with his family. God was actively at work the whole time, even though it may not have seemed like it.

You might want everything fixed right now, but remember that God takes His time. He has important lessons to teach in your waiting. Trust Him and His timing. He knows what He is doing.

LORD JESUS, I BRING MY BROKEN RELATIONSHIPS TO YOU. I RELEASE THEM INTO YOUR LOVING HANDS.

LEAH

When the LORD *saw that Leah was unloved, he enabled her to have children, but Rachel could not conceive.*

GENESIS 29:31 NLT

Jacob was in love with Rachel. He made a deal with Rachel's father, Laban, to marry her after seven years of work. But Laban deceived Jacob. After the wedding feast, Laban waited until dark to bring his older daughter, Leah, to Jacob instead of bringing Rachel to him. Jacob didn't realize the trick until he had already consummated a marriage with the oldest daughter.

The Bible tells us that Leah had "weak eyes," but that her sister, Rachel, was very beautiful (Genesis 29:17 NIV). Laban created a terribly unfair situation for his daughters and Jacob. Jacob never truly loved Leah, although he did father her children. Leah was completely humiliated; she knew how Jacob felt about her sister.

Genesis 29:32 (AMP) says, "Leah conceived and gave birth to a son and named him Reuben (See, a son!), for she said, 'Because the LORD has seen my humiliation and suffering.'"

God saw Leah and cared for her broken heart. He opened her womb and gave her children to love.

HEAVENLY FATHER, THANK YOU FOR SEEING ME AND CARING ABOUT MY BROKEN HEART.

HANNAH

Then Hannah prayed: "My heart rejoices in the LORD! The LORD has made me strong. Now I have an answer for my enemies; I rejoice because you rescued me. No one is holy like the LORD! There is no one besides you; there is no Rock like our God."

1 SAMUEL 2:1–2 NLT

This makes zero sense to us today, but in the Old Testament, it was very common for a man to take more than one wife. Hannah was the wife of Elkanah, who was a good husband to her. But he also had another wife who was cruel to Hannah. She was scorned because she couldn't have children. Hannah hated going to the temple because of all the taunting. It grieved her deeply, and she begged God to give her a child. She was so depressed and desperate that she couldn't even eat.

But then Hannah began pouring out her heart to God. She let loose with Him, so much so that the priest thought she was drunk! But as she shared her deepest feelings and desires with God, He gave her great hope. She went away radiant that day. And God answered her prayers and blessed her with a child.

LORD, I KNOW THAT WHEN I'M STRUGGLING, MY FEELINGS AND EMOTIONS ARE ALWAYS SAFE WITH YOU. THANK YOU FOR GIVING ME GREAT HOPE AS I PROCESS MY EMOTIONS WITH YOU!

DANIEL

The king was overjoyed and ordered that Daniel be lifted from the den. Not a scratch was found on him, for he had trusted in his God.

DANIEL 6:23 NLT

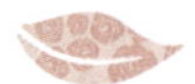

As a young Jewish man, Daniel was taken captive to Babylon and chosen to be among a group of men who would enter the king's service. These men were noble, handsome, and smart (Daniel 1:3–4). The officials offered fine wine and the best food for these trainees. But Daniel and several of his friends refused to partake, choosing instead to remain faithful to God and His laws for them.

The young men's faith was severely tested during their time of training and service, time and time again. (Fiery furnace, anyone?) Yet they remained faithful to the one true God, and He blessed them for it.

Years later, Daniel became a great leader in the land. The other jealous leaders plotted against him, obligating the king to throw him into a den of lions. Was God still with Daniel? Yes, He was. God sent an angel to close the mouths of the lions, so it's quite possible that Daniel even got a great night's sleep! But the king? Not so much (Daniel 6:18)!

We love the same God as Daniel, and He is *always* watching and protecting us in our struggles!

FATHER, HELP ME TO REMAIN FAITHFUL TO YOU DURING DIFFICULT TIMES.

DAVID

Have mercy on me, O God, have mercy! I look to you for protection. I will hide beneath the shadow of your wings until the danger passes by. I cry out to God Most High, to God who will fulfill his purpose for me. He will send help from heaven to rescue me, disgracing those who hound me. . . . My God will send forth his unfailing love and faithfulness.

PSALM 57:1–3 NLT

King Saul was on the hunt. He wanted David dead. David was hiding out in a cave in fear for his life. Psalm 57 is the cry of his heart during that desperate struggle. After David poured out his heart to God and laid out all his fears, he began to praise God and remember all His promises. David said, "For your unfailing love is as high as the heavens. Your faithfulness reaches to the clouds. Be exalted, O God, above the highest heavens. May your glory shine over all the earth" (Psalm 57:10–11 NLT).

Life can get pretty dark sometimes. But there is great power in our prayers as we stand on the promises of God, worshipping in the midst of the darkness. God came through for David that day in the cave (1 Samuel 24), and He'll come through for you too.

I TRUST IN YOUR FAITHFULNESS, FATHER GOD!

DAVID AND GOLIATH

David said to the Philistine, "You come against me with sword and spear and javelin, but I come against you in the name of the LORD Almighty, the God of the armies of Israel, whom you have defied."

1 SAMUEL 17:45 NIV

You probably know this story well. David slew the giant Goliath with a stone from his slingshot. All the other Israelites were terrified of Goliath. No one was willing to fight him except young David, who wasn't even a warrior. Where did David get the courage and strength to do this? Check out his words: "Your servant has been keeping his father's sheep. When a lion or a bear came and carried off a sheep from the flock, I went after it, struck it and rescued the sheep from its mouth. When it turned on me, I seized it by its hair, struck it and killed it. . . . The LORD who rescued me from the paw of the lion and the paw of the bear will rescue me from the hand of this Philistine" (1 Samuel 17:34–35, 37 NIV).

While David was tending sheep, God protected him many times. This shepherd trusted that God would protect him against Goliath too.

When you're struggling to find strength for your struggles, remind yourself of all the times when God has cared for you in the past. And trust that He will do it again!

LORD, I TRUST YOU TO PROVIDE THE COURAGE AND STRENGTH TO OVERCOME THE GIANTS IN MY LIFE.

RUTH

Then the women of the town said to Naomi, "Praise the LORD, who has now provided a redeemer for your family! May this child be famous in Israel. May he restore your youth and care for you in your old age. For he is the son of your daughter-in-law who loves you and has been better to you than seven sons!"

RUTH 4:14–15 NLT

Ruth's husband died. Her mother-in-law, Naomi, was grieving the loss of her husband and two sons. And Ruth would soon be uprooted from her homeland. But she *chose* this path because of faithfulness and commitment to her mother-in-law. In Ruth 1:16 (NLT), she said to her mother-in-law, "Wherever you go, I will go; wherever you live, I will live. Your people will be my people, and your God will be my God."

And Ruth was true to her word. She was committed to Naomi, honoring her and taking her advice. She chose to follow God as well, and He blessed her. Even though she had to work very hard at first, gleaning in the fields, God saw Ruth's need, and He already had a plan in the works.

God sent Boaz into the women's lives. He married Ruth, and they became the ancestors of Jesus Himself! What a beautiful story of redemption!

YOU ARE MY REDEEMER, LORD.
I PRAISE YOU FOR WHO YOU ARE.

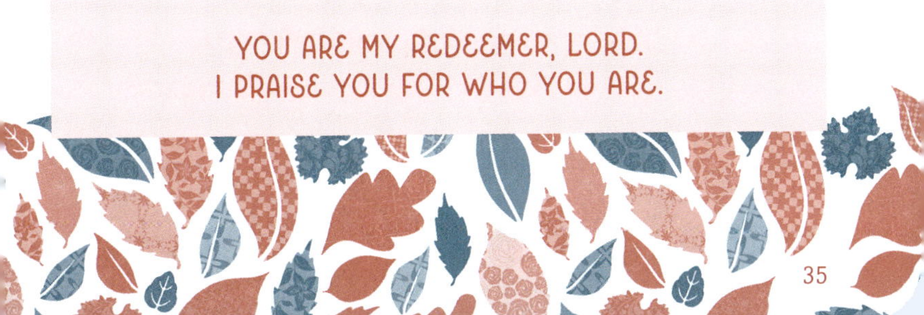

JOB

"The LORD gave me what I had, and the LORD has taken it away. Praise the name of the LORD!"

JOB 1:21 NLT

Job was a wealthy landowner who loved God. But Satan accused Job of loving God only because of the good life he had. And then Job's trials began. He lost nearly everything. His children were killed, his livestock raided and destroyed, his home ruined. He was left with a wife who told him to "curse God and die" (Job 2:9) and three toxic friends. Talk about struggles!

In the end, God restored Job, blessed him, and rebuked his friends. In all of Job's trials, he didn't lose his faith in God. But he did question God's reasoning. God answered Job's questions about human suffering with two chapters of questions of His own (Job 38–39), beginning with, "Where were you when I laid the earth's foundation?" (38:4 NIV).

We can't fully comprehend the mind of God. We don't know everything. First Corinthians 13:12 (NLT) explains: "Now we see things imperfectly, like puzzling reflections in a mirror, but then we will see everything with perfect clarity. All that I know now is partial and incomplete, but then I will know everything completely, just as God now knows me completely."

LORD, EVEN THOUGH I DON'T FULLY UNDERSTAND YOU, I TRUST YOUR GOODNESS.

ELIJAH

Then the hand of the Lord came upon Elijah [giving him supernatural strength]. He girded up his loins and outran Ahab to the entrance of Jezreel [nearly twenty miles].

1 Kings 18:46 AMP

Elijah was a prophet who obeyed God, but not everyone was happy with him for speaking truth and exposing their wickedness. He condemned idol worship and called God's people to return to Him. The king's wife, Jezebel, wanted Elijah dead. But God protected His courageous, obedient servant. He caused a heavy rain to fall and gave Elijah supernatural strength and speed to outrun King Ahab's horses.

You may hear some Christians say that God doesn't work like that anymore. But the Bible says that God is the same yesterday, today, and forever (Hebrews 13:8). The same protector and sustainer of Elijah is your God too. Maybe you won't get up and run super fast to save the day (although the adrenaline God gave us has been known to cause similar, modern-day miracles), but you can rest assured that the God of all creation can give you renewed strength in creative ways. He can do what He has always done and show up in powerful ways in your life.

LORD, FORGIVE ME FOR THE TIMES I'VE DOUBTED YOUR POWER IN MY LIFE. I WANT TO KNOW YOU AND TRUST YOU MORE.

ELIJAH'S DEPRESSION

Then he went on alone into the wilderness, traveling all day. He sat down under a solitary broom tree and prayed that he might die. "I have had enough, Lord," he said. "Take my life, for I am no better than my ancestors who have already died." Then he lay down and slept under the broom tree. But as he was sleeping, an angel touched him and told him, "Get up and eat!"

1 Kings 19:4–5 NLT

After all the running and traveling, Elijah collapsed. He was so done with his exhausting, difficult life that He asked God to let him die. Can you imagine the despair he was feeling?

But God saw Elijah. He didn't reprimand him or tell him that he just needed more faith. No. What did God do? He tenderly cared for Elijah. God knew exactly what Elijah needed, so He sent an angel to feed and minister to him. (A nap and a good meal made by someone else can make all the difference sometimes. Yes?)

God is our ever-present help in time of need. We can hide away in Him. And He gives us the supernatural help we need to get back up and running again.

I'M TIRED TOO, LORD. HELP ME TRUST THAT YOU'LL CARE FOR ALL MY NEEDS.

MARY

Gabriel appeared to her and said, "Greetings, favored woman! The Lord is with you!" Confused and disturbed, Mary tried to think what the angel could mean. "Don't be afraid, Mary," the angel told her, "for you have found favor with God!"

LUKE 1:28–30 NLT

The story of Christmas is shared each year at Christmas Eve services around the globe. We know it well.

But after hearing the story, have you ever put yourself in Mary's shoes? Imagine the shame you'd feel if you'd kept yourself pure and wound up pregnant! Maybe Mary didn't feel that way at all since the angel had come and fortified her faith. But getting others to believe her? That was quite a challenge. Plus, she was so young. The Bible doesn't say how old Mary was when she became pregnant, but most historians believe that she was a very young teenager. But even at her young age, we know this about Mary: God chose her, and He had a redemptive plan.

Mary went through some very difficult times in her life, but she chose to trust God through all of it. Luke 1:38 (NIV) says, "'I am the Lord's servant,' Mary answered. 'May your word to me be fulfilled.' Then the angel left her."

God planned for Mary to be encouraged by her cousin Elizabeth, who believed her and took her in.

THANK YOU FOR YOUR REDEMPTIVE PLAN, LORD. I BELIEVE YOU ALWAYS MAKE A WAY.

PAUL

Because of the surpassing greatness and extraordinary nature of the revelations [which I received from God], for this reason, to keep me from thinking of myself as important, a thorn in the flesh was given to me, a messenger of Satan, to torment and harass me—to keep me from exalting myself!

2 CORINTHIANS 12:7 AMP

The apostle Paul had been a Pharisee who hated followers of Jesus. That is, until the moment that Jesus Himself called to him. This interaction changed Paul's life forever, and he spent the rest of his days serving Jesus and proclaiming the truth of the gospel.

Still, Paul had many struggles. He had a "thorn in the flesh" that he begged God to take away. But God's answer was no. Paul believed that God wanted to keep him reliant on His power instead of becoming conceited and proud (2 Corinthians 12:9–10). Sometimes God says no to our prayers because He knows there's something better for us. He sees things we can't.

After everything Paul had gone through, he was still able to say, "Praise be to the God and Father of our Lord Jesus Christ, who has blessed us in the heavenly realms with every spiritual blessing in Christ" (Ephesians 1:3 NIV).

LORD, HELP ME TRUST THAT YOU SEE WHAT IS BEST FOR ME EVEN WHEN I DON'T UNDERSTAND. THANK YOU FOR EVERY BLESSING I HAVE IN CHRIST!

TELL YOURSELF THE TRUTH

"Then you will know the truth, and the truth will set you free."

John 8:32 NIV

If the first thing on your mind when you wake up is your overwhelming to-do list and it stresses you out, you should start your day over. God wants you to know the truth about who you are and who He is. When your heart and mind are aligned with Him and His truth, those daily stressors don't seem so bad anymore.

Write some of your favorite scriptures down and post them on your bedside table. Get in the habit of telling yourself the truth before you start your day. Let's start with these powerful promises from scripture:

- I am a child of God, and the evil one can't touch me (1 John 5:18).
- I am free and clean in the blood of Christ (1 John 1:7; Galatians 5:1).
- God has rescued me from darkness and has brought me into His kingdom (Colossians 1:13).
- I am Christ's friend (John 15:15).
- Nothing can separate me from God's love (Romans 8:38–39).
- God is for me, not against me (Romans 8:31).

LORD, PLANT THESE TRUTHS DEEP IN MY HEART AS I START EACH DAY.

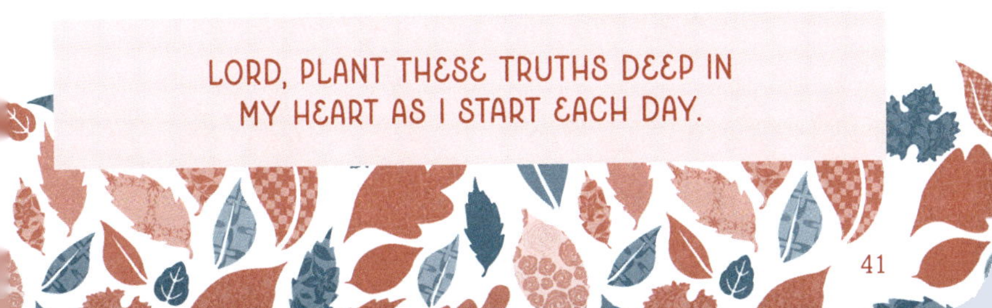

ALL MY ANXIETY

Casting all your cares [all your anxieties, all your worries, and all your concerns, once and for all] on Him, for He cares about you [with deepest affection, and watches over you very carefully].

1 PETER 5:7 AMP

Women tend to carry a lot of their anxiety and struggles in their necks and upper backs. Worry weighs them down in those areas.

How about you? Do you carry worry and anxiety around with you? Where do you feel it in your body?

Try this: Close your eyes and focus on where you feel the anxiety in your body. Then whisper this truth out loud: "I'm casting all my anxiety on Jesus because He cares for me." Ask Jesus to help you give it over to Him. Picture yourself releasing the anxiety you carry. Then quiet yourself in God's presence. Ask Him what He wants you to understand about your anxiety and how best to handle it. Wait and listen for His answer.

When you try this prayer exercise, you may be surprised at what God shows you. A scripture may come to mind. A familiar song or a sermon might pop into your head. God might use your imagination to give you a vision to hold on to. Allow the Holy Spirit to speak to you in whatever way He chooses.

LORD, THANK YOU FOR CARING ABOUT ME SO DEEPLY AND WATCHING OVER ME VERY CAREFULLY.

REPRESENTATIVE WARFARE

"No weapon forged against you will prevail, and you will refute every tongue that accuses you. This is the heritage of the servants of the LORD, and this is their vindication from me," declares the LORD.

ISAIAH 54:17 NIV

In the Old Testament, some of the battles were fought as "representative warfare." This meant that instead of losing many soldiers to war, they would choose one representative from each army to battle each other, and whoever won was the overall victor. That's why David was fighting Goliath one-on-one.

As a child of God, you are never required to summon courage from your own resources and head out into the world, fists swinging (though we all do that from time to time!). We forget about our "heritage" as servants of the Lord. We forget that He will fight our battles for us. He wants to be your representative in the war of daily life.

Commit these truths to memory:

- "This is what the LORD says to you: 'Do not be afraid or discouraged because of this vast army. For the battle is not yours, but God's'" (2 Chronicles 20:15 NIV).
- "Contend, LORD, with those who contend with me; fight against those who fight against me" (Psalm 35:1 NIV).

I BELIEVE YOU ARE WITH ME, JESUS. AND I TRUST THAT NO WEAPON FORMED AGAINST ME WILL PROSPER.

MY DEFENSE ATTORNEY

When they cry out to the Lord because of their oppressors,
he will send them a savior and defender, and he will rescue them.

Isaiah 19:20 NIV

Not only is Jesus your representative warrior in battle, but He is also your defense attorney—the *perfect* defense attorney. Hopefully you've never needed one of those in real life, but if you're ever accused of a crime, you're going to want a defense attorney who knows his stuff!

How about if the Creator of the universe represented and defended you? Isaiah 51:22 tells us that God defends His people. And Jeremiah 50:34 (NIV) says this: "Yet their Redeemer is strong; the Lord Almighty is his name. He will vigorously defend their cause."

You may not be in a legal battle, but you will likely face gossip and lies spread about you at some point in your life. The natural thing to do is defend yourself and try to dispute every lie. But sometimes the issue is just too big. You need Jesus, your perfect defense attorney, to protect and defend you against all the lies. Allow Him to bring the truth to light in His way and in His timing.

LORD, I SURRENDER THIS PROBLEM AND MY REPUTATION TO YOU. PLEASE DEFEND ME AS I HUMBLY SUBMIT MYSELF TO YOUR WILL AND YOUR WAYS.

STRENGTH DURING ILLNESS

My health may fail, and my spirit may grow weak,
but God remains the strength of my heart; he is mine forever.
PSALM 73:26 NLT

If you or a loved one has gone through any kind of lengthy illness, you know how easy it is to lose hope. Day after day of feeling unwell can lead to dark depression.

The Psalms are a good place to hang out when you're in this place. Allow these scriptures to encourage your soul:

- "In peace I will lie down and sleep, for you alone, LORD, make me dwell in safety" (Psalm 4:8 NIV).
- "You, LORD, keep my lamp burning; my God turns my darkness into light" (Psalm 18:28 NIV).
- "The LORD is near to all who call on him, to all who call on him in truth. He fulfills the desires of those who fear him; he hears their cry and saves them" (Psalm 145:18–19 NIV).
- "He will call on me, and I will answer him; I will be with him in trouble, I will deliver him and honor him. With long life I will satisfy him and show him my salvation" (Psalm 91:15–16 NIV).

Just FYI: Psalm 91 makes for great bedtime reading!

PLEASE GIVE ME STRENGTH AS I SATURATE MYSELF WITH YOUR WORD, LORD!

COME TO ME FIRST

"Is anyone thirsty? Come and drink. . . . Come to me with your ears wide open. Listen, and you will find life."

ISAIAH 55:1, 3 NLT

When you're experiencing a chronic illness, you want answers and relief. It's tempting to spend hours chasing down every symptom online. Do you need medication? Or maybe a new supplement or two—or ten—would fix things. Anxiety builds as you read more and more about your condition. With your head spinning and eyes burning, you finally take a break from it all.

A wise friend of mine once shared that when you spend your time trying to control everything, you are aligning yourself with the world instead of with God and His kingdom. Are medications and supplements okay? Of course they are. We have grace and freedom as believers. But when we constantly run to secular websites to get answers about our bodies that God designed instead of going to Him first, we have it backward.

Jesus wants us to go to Him first—for *everything*. He will lead us in the right direction and to the right people to care for us in our time of need.

LORD, TEACH ME TO COME TO YOU FIRST IN MY QUEST FOR PHYSICAL STRENGTH. LEAD ME IN THE RIGHT DIRECTION.

PHYSICAL PAIN

My heart pounds, my strength fails me;
even the light has gone from my eyes.
PSALM 38:10 NIV

David was crying out to God yet again in Psalm 38: "My back is filled with searing pain; there is no health in my body. I am feeble and utterly crushed; I groan in anguish of heart" (verses 7–8 NIV).

Physical pain gets our attention fast. Maybe that's why David said, "LORD, do not forsake me; do not be far from me, my God. Come quickly to help me, my Lord and my Savior" (verses 21–22 NIV).

It's possible to ignore others' problems. You can try to ignore what's going on in the world. But you just can't ignore your own physical pain.

In Psalm 38, David was in a lot of pain. God had his full attention. David realized that his own sin had caused his pain and isolation (verse 5). But he confessed and repented in verse 18 (NLT): "But I confess my sins; I am deeply sorry for what I have done."

Know this, friend: Physical pain is not always caused by our own sin (see John 9:2–3). But sometimes we do contribute to the unhealthy state of our bodies because of our poor choices. Is there anything you need to get right with Jesus?

SEARCH MY HEART AND MIND, LORD JESUS. SHOW ME ANYTHING THAT I NEED TO BRING TO YOU IN REPENTANCE.

YOU ARE NOT ALONE

Have mercy on me, Lord, for I am in distress. Tears blur my eyes. My body and soul are withering away. I am dying from grief; my years are shortened by sadness. Sin has drained my strength; I am wasting away from within.

Psalm 31:9–10 NLT

The Psalms have a way of getting to the heart of the matter, exposing the depths of our feelings. Can you relate? Psalm 31 is a great place to linger when you're experiencing struggles and grief.

You are not alone—even if it feels like you are. Even when the enemy whispers lies and you feel isolated, like you are the only one going through something hard. Don't give the lies and dark thoughts any space in your head.

Trust that God sees you. Your times are in His hands (31:15). He stores up goodness for His people (verse 19). He keeps you safe from your accusers (verse 20).

Psalm 31:7 (AMP) says, "I will rejoice and be glad in Your steadfast love, because You have seen my affliction; You have taken note of my life's distresses."

HEAVENLY FATHER, I CHOOSE TO BELIEVE YOUR WORD. I TRUST THAT YOU SEE ME AND THAT YOU'VE TAKEN NOTE OF MY STRUGGLES AND DISTRESS. I WON'T BELIEVE THE ENEMY'S LIES! I AM NOT ALONE.

ABIDING IN CHRIST

The Lord *will give [unyielding and impenetrable] strength to His people; the* Lord *will bless His people with peace.*

Psalm 29:11 AMP

The strength God gives His people is not human strength—it's supernatural, "unyielding and impenetrable," and available only to those of us who abide in Christ. John 15:4–5 (NLT) says, "Remain in me, and I will remain in you. For a branch cannot produce fruit if it is severed from the vine, and you cannot be fruitful unless you remain in me. Yes, I am the vine; you are the branches. Those who remain in me, and I in them, will produce much fruit. For apart from me you can do nothing."

Did you catch that last part? We can do *nothing* apart from Christ—nothing that makes a difference in the kingdom. Nothing that changes the lives of the people around us for the better. We cannot produce good fruit apart from abiding and remaining in the vine.

We have supernatural strength available to us at all times but only as we abide and make our home in Christ. Get into His Word, start listening for His voice, and stay close to Jesus.

I WANT THE STRENGTH THAT YOU OFFER, LORD JESUS. TEACH ME HOW TO ABIDE IN YOU.

WHEN YOU FAIL

You, Lord. . .are my strength; come quickly to help me.

Psalm 22:19 NIV

Sometimes our bodies and minds just give out. We get it wrong. We make a mess of things. We fall hard. We fail.

When this kind of thing happens again and again, it's easy to see ourselves as failures. But take encouragement from God's Word:

- "The godly may trip seven times, but they will get up again. But one disaster is enough to overthrow the wicked" (Proverbs 24:16 NLT).
- "The Lord helps the fallen and lifts those bent beneath their loads" (Psalm 145:14 NLT).
- "If we confess our sins, he is faithful and just and will forgive us our sins and purify us from all unrighteousness" (1 John 1:9 NIV).
- "God has united you with Christ Jesus. For our benefit God made him to be wisdom itself. Christ made us right with God; he made us pure and holy, and he freed us from sin" (1 Corinthians 1:30 NLT).
- "Therefore, if anyone is in Christ, the new creation has come: The old has gone, the new is here!" (2 Corinthians 5:17 NIV).

HEAVENLY FATHER, THANK YOU FOR MAKING ME A NEW CREATION IN CHRIST!

STRUGGLING WITH FEAR

"For the LORD your God is going with you! He will fight for you against your enemies, and he will give you victory!"

DEUTERONOMY 20:4 NLT

Spiritual warfare is real. Ephesians 6:12 (NIV) says, "For our struggle is not against flesh and blood, but against the rulers, against the authorities, against the powers of this dark world and against the spiritual forces of evil in the heavenly realms."

The Bible tells us to be alert because our enemy prowls around looking to devour us (1 Peter 5:8). The Bible also tells us that our battle exists in the "unseen world" (Ephesians 6:12 NLT). God tells us this not so we'll be afraid but rather so we'll be aware.

Do you ever struggle with fear? Fear can be a very difficult battle for a woman, and it is one of our enemy's main schemes against us. But God has given us everything we need to overcome. We don't fight in our own strength. No. He fights for us.

Isaiah 41:10 (NIV) says, "So do not fear, for I am with you; do not be dismayed, for I am your God. I will strengthen you and help you; I will uphold you with my righteous right hand."

HOLY SPIRIT, HELP ME COMMIT THIS VERSE TO MEMORY SO I WILL NOT FEAR. I TRUST YOU TO STRENGTHEN AND HELP ME!

SHIELDED BY GOD

The L*ORD* *is my strength and my shield;*
my heart trusts in him, and he helps me. My heart
leaps for joy, and with my song I praise him.

PSALM 28:7 NIV

When you allow Jesus to be your strength, He also becomes your shield. The Hebrew word for shield is *magen*. Strong's Concordance also says it can mean "armed," "defense," and like "the scaly hide of the crocodile." God created crocodiles with bumpy skin that protects them from harm. One look at a crocodile, and people and predators know to stay away!

Let God shield you like that during your struggles. He is a hiding place. You can always run to Him for anything. With His mighty power, He shields you from anything coming against you (Isaiah 54:17).

If God is your shield and protector, nothing can get through that armor unless it serves His purpose. And if He does allow something difficult to break through, He will provide the strength you need to fight that battle. Psalm 59:9–10 (NIV) says, "You are my strength, I watch for you; you, God, are my fortress, my God on whom I can rely."

I NEED YOU TO SHIELD ME, GOD.
THIS ALL FEELS TOO HARD. SHOW ME
WHAT IT MEANS TO HIDE MYSELF IN YOU.

PRAISE IN THE STRUGGLE

But I will sing of your strength, in the morning I will sing of your love; for you are my fortress, my refuge in times of trouble. You are my strength, I sing praise to you; you, God, are my fortress, my God on whom I can rely.

PSALM 59:16–17 NIV

Encouraging words from a friend can do wonders during a difficult time. Our family was once sick with the flu. We'd been down for a few weeks and kept passing our germs around. One family member would feel better, and then another one would succumb to the illness.

A friend from church reached out to us and sent an image of Psalm 139:14 (NIV), which says, "I praise you because I am fearfully and wonderfully made; your works are wonderful, I know that full well." Her text said, "I am so sorry that you have been sick so long. You may not feel so wonderfully made, but you are! May you have a breakthrough in your health today just like the sun broke through the clouds."

That made a world of difference in my attitude that day and ever since! I was able to praise during the struggle and thank God for my amazing body, which He created.

The Message says, "Body and soul, I am marvelously made! I worship in adoration—what a creation!" (Psalm 139:14).

I PRAISE YOU IN THE STRUGGLES, LORD!

STRUGGLES WITH PEOPLE

My soul is weary with sorrow;
strengthen me according to your word.
PSALM 119:28 NIV

How many times has your soul been "weary with sorrow" because of other people hurting you? Forgiveness is a touchy subject, and yet Jesus calls us to do it (Matthew 18).

Forgiveness can be a long process sometimes, especially in the case of abuse and betrayal. We're called to forgive so that we don't carry that bitterness throughout our lives. But here's the thing that can get mixed up in the church: Forgiveness and reconciliation are not the same thing. Forgiveness doesn't mean you sweep everything under the rug and pretend like nothing happened. Forgiveness is releasing the issue and the person into God's hands and allowing Him to be the judge.

God isn't telling you to trust people who've repeatedly wronged you. He isn't saying you have to stay in relationship with toxic and abusive people. Forgive and release them into His hands? Yes. Trust them? No.

If you're struggling with forgiveness, bring it all to Jesus. Allow His strength to help you release the person into His hands.

I WANT TO BE FREE FROM BITTERNESS, LORD. SHOW ME HOW TO FORGIVE THOSE WHO'VE HARMED ME!

GOD'S EYES

"The eyes of the LORD *search the whole earth in order to strengthen those whose hearts are fully committed to him."*

2 CHRONICLES 16:9 NLT

When my daughter was little, she enjoyed playing with her Barbie Dreamhouse that a friend had given us. She loved looking in at all the dolls in the various rooms included in the four-story home. The wind-up elevator was especially fun.

One day we were driving, and she was thinking about her Dreamhouse. She wondered out loud if the Dreamhouse was kind of like God's eyes looking in at all of us in the world. Deep thoughts from a five-year-old!

God is looking lovingly upon you too, friend. The Bible has more to say about God's eyes. Check out these scripture verses:

- "Nothing in all creation is hidden from God's sight. Everything is uncovered and laid bare before the eyes of him to whom we must give account" (Hebrews 4:13 NIV).
- "For the eyes of the Lord are on the righteous and his ears are attentive to their prayer, but the face of the Lord is against those who do evil" (1 Peter 3:12 NIV).

God sees all. He cares about you. And if your heart is fully committed to Him, then He wants to strengthen you!

I'M THANKFUL THAT YOU SEE ME, LORD.
THANK YOU FOR WANTING TO STRENGTHEN ME!

THE STRENGTH GOD PROVIDES

If anyone serves, they should do so with the strength God provides, so that in all things God may be praised through Jesus Christ. To him be the glory and the power for ever and ever. Amen.

1 Peter 4:11 NIV

People sometimes claim to do a whole lot of "Christian work" that has nothing to do with God. While well-meaning, churches and pastors and ministry leaders can get distracted just like anyone else. And then they have the enemy of their mission to contend with—an enemy who wants to thwart all their efforts and cause disaster.

The Bible tells us that when we are serving God, we need to be particularly careful to do it only in the strength God provides, not in our own strength—so He alone gets the glory! Not us, not our ministry, not our program.

All of us are called to be servants in God's kingdom! Are you doing so out of your own strength or God's? Think of any ministries in which you are currently serving. How's that going for you? Do you feel frazzled and hurried? Running on empty? Bring your ministry before Jesus. Surrender it to Him. Ask Him to fill you with His mission and strength so He alone gets the glory!

LORD, PLEASE HELP ME TO SERVE OUT OF THE STRENGTH THAT YOU PROVIDE. ALL GLORY TO YOU!

WEAKNESS TURNED TO STRENGTH

By faith these people overthrew kingdoms, ruled with justice, and received what God had promised them. They shut the mouths of lions, quenched the flames of fire, and escaped death by the edge of the sword. Their weakness was turned to strength. They became strong in battle and put whole armies to flight.

HEBREWS 11:33–34 NLT

Hebrews 11 is the Bible's "Hall of Faith." It details the lives of the giants of the faith throughout the Old Testament. These people faced enormous struggle and adversity. Their weakness was turned to strength because of their faith, and their stories have encouraged the family of believers throughout the generations.

Hebrews 11:6 (NLT) says, "It is impossible to please God without faith. Anyone who wants to come to him must believe that God exists and that he rewards those who sincerely seek him." *The Message* paraphrases it this way: "It's impossible to please God apart from faith. And why? Because anyone who wants to approach God must believe both that he exists and that he cares enough to respond to those who seek him."

God cares for you. His love for you is everlasting. And His strength is always enough.

LORD, HELP ME TO TRUST YOU LIKE THE GIANTS OF THE FAITH DID. I BRING YOU MY WEAKNESS. PLEASE TURN IT INTO STRENGTH TO DO WHAT YOU HAVE CALLED ME TO DO.

WHEN PEOPLE DESERT YOU

At my first defense, no one came to my support, but everyone deserted me. May it not be held against them. But the Lord stood at my side and gave me strength, so that through me the message might be fully proclaimed and all the Gentiles might hear it. And I was delivered from the lion's mouth.

2 TIMOTHY 4:16–17 NIV

Paul was probably feeling lonely when he wrote this letter to Timothy. In 2 Timothy 4:10, Paul mentioned the people who had deserted him. And in verse 16, he shared that no one showed up to support him.

Ever feel like that? Like no one's got you? Maybe it's not intentional and it's just the busyness of life keeping good friends and family away in your time of need. But it sure does feel lonely, doesn't it? And in that feeling of loneliness, the enemy likes to get in your head and whisper lies. Don't fall for it! Paul said that when he felt deserted, the Lord Himself stood by his side and gave him strength.

If you're feeling deserted, reach out to Jesus. Take a leap of faith. Let God Himself come to support and speak to you.

LORD, I NEED YOUR SUPPORT AND LOVE DURING THIS TIME OF STRUGGLE. REMIND ME THAT YOU ARE HERE WITH ME!

UNDER ATTACK

But the Lord is faithful, and he will strengthen you and protect you from the evil one.
2 THESSALONIANS 3:3 NIV

There are certain times in life where it seems like everything that could possibly go wrong does go wrong. As we know from God's Word, spiritual warfare is real. It could very well be that you are under attack. Should you be afraid? No! You can fight back through the strength of Christ Himself and the power of His Word.

When you feel like you're up against unusual and alarming circumstances, repeat God's truth!

- "You, dear children, are from God and have overcome them, because the one who is in you is greater than the one who is in the world" (1 John 4:4 NIV).
- "The thief comes only to steal and kill and destroy; I have come that they may have life, and have it to the full" (John 10:10 NIV).
- "The One who was born of God keeps them safe, and the evil one cannot harm them" (1 John 5:18 NIV).
- "Submit yourselves, then, to God. Resist the devil, and he will flee from you" (James 4:7 NIV).

Isaiah 54:17; Psalm 91:1; and Psalm 119:105 are also great to add to this list!

LORD, I WILL HIDE YOUR WORD IN MY HEART AND SPEAK YOUR TRUTH OVER MY CIRCUMSTANCES.

BLESSING IN DISGUISE

Dear brothers and sisters, when troubles of any kind come your way, consider it an opportunity for great joy. For you know that when your faith is tested, your endurance has a chance to grow.

JAMES 1:2–3 NLT

It's not fun to hear someone speak the words "everything happens for a reason" when you're going through hard times. It can seem harsh and lacking in empathy. But have you ever been in the middle of difficulty and a quiet whisper comes at you seemingly from nowhere: *Hey! Maybe this hard thing is a blessing. Dig a little deeper.*

Perhaps you're dealing with an illness or a complete change of long-term plans at the last minute. Whatever the case may be, press in and search for God's heart in all of it. Maybe this is a holy interruption.

Are God's plans for you good? Yes! So you can trust that whatever is happening right now is for your good and His glory. A detour may lead you to a divine appointment. A sick day—or even a sick week—may be God's protection in some way you can't see yet. What seems like a huge inconvenience today might end up being one of the best things to happen in your life!

LORD, I TRUST THAT YOU'RE AT WORK IN THE MIDDLE OF MY DIFFICULTIES. CHANGE MY HEART TO SEE THE BLESSINGS.

GIVING UP CONTROL

My old self has been crucified with Christ. It is no longer I who live, but Christ lives in me. So I live in this earthly body by trusting in the Son of God, who loved me and gave himself for me.

GALATIANS 2:20 NLT

Control is often a trauma response. People who feel like they aren't safe in a situation will often try to control everything. If you find yourself in a power struggle like this, it's wise to get to the bottom of it. Do you have a hard time giving up control? Prayerfully sit with Jesus and ask Him to reveal the "why" behind your control issues.

Use Psalm 139:23–24 (NIV) as your prayer guide: "Search me, God, and know my heart; test me and know my anxious thoughts. See if there is any offensive way in me, and lead me in the way everlasting."

Ask Jesus to highlight any areas where you struggle with control. Why are you hesitant to trust God with your life? What triggers come to mind that cause you to want to have control? Journal anything that He brings to your attention. Repent and allow Jesus to breathe new life into these areas.

JESUS, I REPENT OF MY CONTROLLING BEHAVIOR. YOU ARE ALIVE IN ME, AND I WANT TO TRUST YOU IN WAYS THAT I HAVEN'T BEFORE.

LETTING GO OF PRIDE

"God opposes the proud but gives grace to the humble."
JAMES 4:6 NLT

Pride rears its ugly head every day. The Bible tells us there are some things that God really hates: "These six things the LORD hates; indeed, seven are repulsive to Him: a proud look [the attitude that makes one overestimate oneself and discount others], a lying tongue, and hands that shed innocent blood, a heart that creates wicked plans, feet that run swiftly to evil, a false witness who breathes out lies [even half-truths], and one who spreads discord (rumors) among brothers" (Proverbs 6:16–19 AMP).

Struggling with any of those things? Ouch. There it is in black and white—what God thinks about it. How often are we guilty of being selfish? Overestimating ourselves and our abilities and discounting others? Pride can be insidious too. It's right there staring back at you in the mirror, but you can't even see it.

Jesus calls us to die to ourselves (Matthew 16:24), and that can be a daily, hourly, sometimes even moment-by-moment struggle! Trust that God wants to give you the strength to overcome. Bring your pride to Jesus every morning and surrender it to Him.

LORD, I REPENT OF MY SIN OF PRIDE.
I NEED SO MUCH HELP WITH THIS!

ASKING FOR HELP

From Him the whole body [the church, in all its various parts], joined and knitted firmly together by what every joint supplies, when each part is working properly, causes the body to grow and mature, building itself up in [unselfish] love.

EPHESIANS 4:16 AMP

For some of us, one of the biggest struggles we have is asking for help when we need it. Why is this so? Control issues and pride can create so many problems. Or perhaps you just don't want to bother anyone else with your troubles.

Always ask for help from Jesus first. Listen as He makes a way for you. He will point you in the right direction. He will soften the hearts of the people whom He wants to use in your life. Allow the body of Christ to *be* the body of Christ.

The Message creatively words Ephesians 4:15–16: "We take our lead from Christ, who is the source of everything we do. He keeps us in step with each other. His very breath and blood flow through us, nourishing us so that we will grow up healthy in God, robust in love."

With Christ's life flowing through us, He wants us to help one another in unselfish love. So, reach out when you have a need. Let God's people do their job.

LORD, HELP ME LAY DOWN MY HESITATIONS AND ASK FOR HELP WHEN YOU PROMPT ME.

CULTURAL INFLUENCE

But now he has reconciled you by Christ's physical body through death to present you holy in his sight, without blemish and free from accusation—if you continue in your faith, established and firm, and do not move from the hope held out in the gospel.

COLOSSIANS 1:22–23 NIV

Because of Jesus' sacrifice for you on the cross—His death, resurrection, and ascension into heaven—you have full access to God. He looks at you as holy, without any blemishes, completely free from accusation. He loves you so much that He made a way for you to be with Him for eternity. This is the gospel.

Our world is full of chaos and confusion, and if you're not hanging tight to Jesus and His Word, you can get confused and swept up in the culture. If you find that you're struggling with the pull that our culture has on you, ask God for help. As His Spirit convicts you, spend less time online and on social media. Ask for opportunities to share His love with your family and friends and people in your community.

Let God and His Word influence you more than the culture.

LORD, HELP ME TO LISTEN FOR YOUR CONVICTION AS I INTERACT WITH OUR CULTURE. I WANT YOUR WORD TO INFLUENCE ME MORE THAN ANYTHING ELSE.

STRENGTH DURING SUFFERING

And the God of all grace, who called you to his eternal glory in Christ, after you have suffered a little while, will himself restore you and make you strong, firm and steadfast.

1 PETER 5:10 NIV

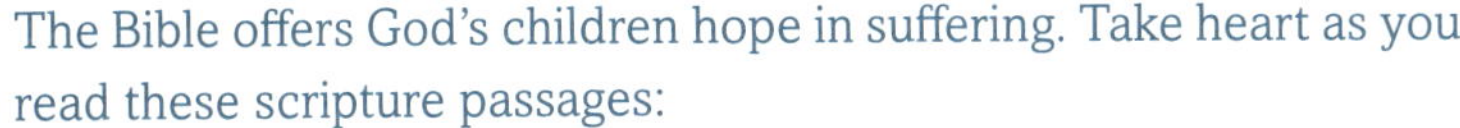

The Bible offers God's children hope in suffering. Take heart as you read these scripture passages:

- "For I consider [from the standpoint of faith] that the sufferings of the present life are not worthy to be compared with the glory that is about to be revealed to us and in us! For [even the whole] creation [all nature] waits eagerly for the children of God to be revealed" (Romans 8:18–19 AMP).
- "'I have told you these things, so that in Me you may have [perfect] peace. In the world you have tribulation and distress and suffering, but be courageous [be confident, be undaunted, be filled with joy]; I have overcome the world.' [My conquest is accomplished, My victory abiding.]" (John 16:33 AMP).
- "'He will wipe every tear from their eyes. There will be no more death' or mourning or crying or pain, for the old order of things has passed away" (Revelation 21:4 NIV).

THANK YOU FOR THE ENCOURAGEMENT
I FIND IN YOUR WORD, LORD.

HELP!

We can rejoice, too, when we run into problems and trials, for we know that they help us develop endurance. And endurance develops strength of character, and character strengthens our confident hope of salvation. And this hope will not lead to disappointment. For we know how dearly God loves us, because he has given us the Holy Spirit to fill our hearts with his love.

ROMANS 5:3–5 NLT

When you're dealing with troubles and heartache, looking for the silver lining can be tough. Especially when, day after day, you wake up and things are *still* hard. A difficult marriage. A child who is breaking your heart. An illness. A job that sucks the life out of you.

But when you're a child of God, no matter how bad things may seem, there's *always* hope. So, if you're struggling today, lift your head, friend. That silver lining is there—you just have to be willing to look for it. Start today.

What if you began praying, asking God to change things? Even if you struggle with doubt, what if you just decided to begin asking for His help?

God loves you so much. He longs to pour His Spirit into your heart, and He will—if you let Him.

I NEED YOUR HELP AND STRENGTH DURING MY STRUGGLES, LORD.

PRAYER WORKS

"Call to Me and I will answer you, and tell you [and even show you] great and mighty things, [things which have been confined and hidden], which you do not know and understand and cannot distinguish."

JEREMIAH 33:3 AMP

God's Word has a lot to say about prayer. Check out these scriptures:

- "Then you will call on me and come and pray to me, and I will listen to you" (Jeremiah 29:12 NIV).
- "If you remain in me and my words remain in you, ask whatever you wish, and it will be done for you" (John 15:7 NIV).
- "This is the confidence we have in approaching God: that if we ask anything according to his will, he hears us" (1 John 5:14 NIV).
- "For this reason I am telling you, whatever things you ask for in prayer [in accordance with God's will], believe [with confident trust] that you have received them, and they will be given to you" (Mark 11:24 AMP).

If you've been struggling to believe that prayer really makes a difference, reach out to the heavenly Father. Ask Him to strengthen your faith. He can, and He will!

LORD, TEACH ME TO PRAY ACCORDING TO YOUR WILL.

MORE THAN MEETS THE EYE

For our light and momentary troubles are achieving for us an eternal glory that far outweighs them all.

2 CORINTHIANS 4:17 NIV

Cancer doesn't feel "light and momentary." Separation and divorce don't feel that way either. More like heavy and never ending.

If you're struggling with a serious illness or you're currently in the middle of a messy divorce, you're probably wondering, *How can this verse comfort me in the middle of the worst struggle of my life?*

The Message words 2 Corinthians 4:16–18 like this: "So we're not giving up. How could we! Even though on the outside it often looks like things are falling apart on us, on the inside, where God is making new life, not a day goes by without his unfolding grace. These hard times are small potatoes compared to the coming good times, the lavish celebration prepared for us. There's far more here than meets the eye. The things we see now are here today, gone tomorrow. But the things we can't see now will last forever."

Friend, God is with you. He alone provides the strength you need so you won't give up. God can make you brand new from the inside out! He really is at work doing "more here than meets the eye."

Take a small step of faith today—even if it's just with your pinky toe pointed in God's direction.

LORD, I WANT TO TRUST YOU. I REALLY DO. BUT I'M STRUGGLING. PLEASE HELP MY UNBELIEF (MARK 9:24).

GOD MAKES A WAY

"When you pass through the waters, I will be with you; and when you pass through the rivers, they will not sweep over you. When you walk through the fire, you will not be burned; the flames will not set you ablaze."

ISAIAH 43:2 NIV

In the Old Testament, God's people needed Him to intervene in miraculous ways. And He did! They were enslaved in Egypt, and God provided rescue through the Red Sea, which swallowed up their enemies but not them. In the book of Daniel, Shadrach, Meshach, and Abednego were thrown into a fiery furnace, yet not a hair on their heads was singed!

As Christians today, we have been grafted into God's family because of Jesus (Ephesians 2:13–14). Just as God made a way for His people in the Old Testament, He makes a way for us today.

If you are in a time of struggle, remember who your Father is. He is the all-powerful Creator of the world. Everything is His and He is *for* you. He will be with you in deep water and fire. He can change hearts, minds, and circumstances. And He is with you always.

FATHER, I'M SO THANKFUL TO BE YOUR CHILD! I TRUST THAT YOU WILL MAKE A WAY FOR ME IN MY TIME OF STRUGGLE.

THE BREAKING POINT

Then Job replied to the Lord: "I know that you can do all things; no purpose of yours can be thwarted. You asked, 'Who is this that obscures my plans without knowledge?' Surely I spoke of things I did not understand, things too wonderful for me to know."

Job 42:1–3 NIV

It wouldn't be quite right to write a devotional book about struggles without mentioning Job at least a time or two, would it? That man experienced more struggles than most of us will in our lifetimes!

Job's humanness and suffering finally took him to the breaking point where he demanded answers from God (Job 31:35) about why He had allowed all this suffering.

God spoke to Job and, in a series of questions, basically asked Job if he, as a human, could understand anything God does. Had Job been there when God created the world and marked out the dimensions of the earth (Job 38:4–5)?

Like Job, when we get to a breaking point and cry out to God, He gives us His perspective. And we can say with Job, "I had only heard about you before, but now I have seen you with my own eyes. I take back everything I said, and I sit in dust and ashes to show my repentance" (Job 42:5–6 NLT).

LORD, I REPENT OF DEMANDING ANSWERS FROM YOU IN MY SUFFERING. I WANT TO SEE YOU CLEARLY. HELP ME TO TRUST YOU MORE.

GOOD SUFFERING?

My suffering was good for me, for it taught me to pay attention to your decrees.

PSALM 119:71 NLT

You may be tempted to skip right past today's reading about "good suffering." It sounds kind of cruel, doesn't it? But what if suffering really does produce something good in our lives?

The truth is, God's Word makes no promise of a trouble-free life. In fact, we are promised the opposite—as Christians, we *will* have struggles: "In this world you will have trouble. But take heart! I have overcome the world" (John 16:33 NIV). But the promise of trouble is followed by a second promise—we can have hope, because of Jesus!

What if your suffering creates deep roots of faith? Jeremiah 17:7–8 (NLT) says, "But blessed are those who trust in the LORD and have made the LORD their hope and confidence. They are like trees planted along a riverbank, with roots that reach deep into the water. Such trees are not bothered by the heat or worried by long months of drought. Their leaves stay green, and they never stop producing fruit."

Perhaps your struggle is preparing you for the future so that you can survive and flourish!

LORD, I WANT TO TRUST THAT YOU ARE AT WORK IN MY STRUGGLES. PLEASE USE THESE HARD TIMES TO GROW DEEP ROOTS OF FAITH IN ME.

YOUR SAFE PLACE

The name of the Lord *is a strong fortress;*
the godly run to him and are safe.
Proverbs 18:10 NLT

Trauma counselors often counsel their clients to think of a safe space in their minds. This can be something like a happy memory, a vacation spot, a favorite place to go every day, or a special place in creation—anywhere that feels completely safe in their mind. This helps the trauma victim get to a place in their head where they are able to process difficult memories. Christian counselors who use this method often have their clients invite Jesus into that space to speak truth to them and help them overcome their fears and triggers.

The Bible tells us that God is our safe place. No matter how old you are, God wants to protect you, comfort you, and tell you how loved you are. Sometimes sitting in the quiet with God is the best way to pray—especially when you are going through a very difficult time. Ask Him to fill you with His love as you sit in His presence. Picture yourself sitting close to Jesus, and let Him love you.

LORD JESUS, I NEED YOU TO BE MY SAFE PLACE. THANK YOU FOR LETTING ME KNOW THAT I CAN ALWAYS RUN TO YOU. THANK YOU FOR LOVING ME SO PERFECTLY.

THE SERVANT'S APRON

All of you, dress yourselves in humility as you relate to one another, for "God opposes the proud but gives grace to the humble."

1 PETER 5:5 NLT

The Amplified Bible helps explain this scripture: "All of you, clothe yourselves with humility toward one another [tie on the servant's apron], for God is opposed to the proud [the disdainful, the presumptuous, and He defeats them], but He gives grace to the humble" (1 Peter 5:5).

It's interesting to think about clothing yourself in humility being like tying on a servant's apron. Tying on the servant's apron can be difficult, right? Especially when you're hungry or tired. Most moms do this daily, but even they get tired and need new strength.

Sometimes it's just hard to let others go first. But God promises to take care of all your needs. Anything that God wants for you will happen. You can trust that He's watching out for you and taking care of you. So don't be afraid to tie on the servant's apron to help others and let others go first. You'll be blessed in the process.

LORD, SOMETIMES I STRUGGLE WITH HUMILITY. I NEED YOUR STRENGTH TO TIE ON THE SERVANT'S APRON. HELP ME LEARN TO PUT OTHERS FIRST AS I TRUST YOU TO MEET MY NEEDS.

AN OVERFLOWING LIFE

Whoever has the Son has life; whoever does not have the Son of God does not have life.

1 JOHN 5:12 NIV

As Christians, we are all waiting for Jesus to return so we can physically be with Him for eternity. And there will be a day when Jesus makes all things new and destroys evil forever. But we don't have to wait for heaven to be a part of God's kingdom and live the life Jesus has for us. We don't just have to endure this world as best we can until we get to heaven. Eternal life has already begun!

Jesus wants us to experience abundant and joyful lives right here. John 10:10 (NIV) says, "The thief comes only to steal and kill and destroy; I have come that they may have life, and have it to the full." The Amplified Bible says, "I came that they may have and enjoy life, and have it in abundance [to the full, till it overflows]."

Are you struggling to feel like your life is abundant and joyful? Tell "the thief" to get lost, and ask Jesus to fill you with His joyful and strength-giving life!

LORD, I WANT A HEART THAT OVERFLOWS WITH THE JOY OF KNOWING YOU SO OTHERS CAN SEE WHAT A DIFFERENCE YOU'VE MADE IN MY LIFE! FILL ME, LORD JESUS.

MIXED MESSAGES

If any of you lacks wisdom, you should ask God, who gives generously to all without finding fault, and it will be given to you.

JAMES 1:5 NIV

How many times have you searched for the answer to your problems online? You head to Google, hopeful that the answer to your struggle will miraculously become clear. Hours later you realize you've followed rabbit trails that lead to nothing but confusion.

At times online research might be appropriate. But for wisdom, God wants you to come to Him first. He will generously provide it when you seek Him first. Check out James 3:17 (NIV): "But the wisdom that comes from heaven is first of all pure; then peace-loving, considerate, submissive, full of mercy and good fruit, impartial and sincere." Does that sound like a rabbit trail of confusion?

Have you ever searched for answers online and found information that gave you peace and was impartial and full of good fruit? Often you can find experts saying the exact opposite of each other, and you end up more confused than when you started.

So, friend, take your struggles to Jesus first. Ask Him to lead you to good fruit that you can trust. He is with you in every hardship.

JESUS, I REPENT OF GOING TO GOOGLE FOR WISDOM BEFORE I ASK YOU. I TRUST THAT YOU KNOW WHAT'S BEST FOR ME.

LIVING WATER

"For the Lamb at the center of the throne will be their shepherd; 'he will lead them to springs of living water.' 'And God will wipe away every tear from their eyes.'"

REVELATION 7:17 NIV

Houseplants create a pleasant environment at home and usually require very little care. But if you go too long without giving them a drink, you'll end up with a dead plant on your hands. Have you ever come home to a wilted plant? Sometimes it's not too late, and if you water it right away, it will bounce back to life. It's amazing to see the wilted leaves stand back up after a good drink.

When life's struggles are piling on, it can feel like your whole life is dried up like that wilted plant. You need some life-giving water, pronto! John 4:10 (NIV) says, "Jesus answered [the woman at the well], 'If you knew the gift of God and who it is that asks you for a drink, you would have asked him and he would have given you living water.'"

Jesus is the living water you need—He will bring you back to life. He will wipe the tears from your eyes and set you back on the path to abundant living.

I AM THIRSTY FOR YOU, LORD. BRING ME BACK TO LIFE. PLEASE FILL ME WITH YOUR LIVING WATER!

GOD'S TRAINING

Dear friends, don't be surprised at the fiery trials you are going through, as if something strange were happening to you. Instead, be very glad—for these trials make you partners with Christ in his suffering, so that you will have the wonderful joy of seeing his glory when it is revealed to all the world.

1 PETER 4:12–13 NLT

A friend gave her life to Jesus. At first she was full of joy and couldn't wait to get to church to be with other believers. But then some problems started coming her way. Her faith was new, and she hadn't developed deep roots yet. She was discouraged. She thought the Christian life was supposed to be better than what she was experiencing.

But what she didn't know is that God was training her. He wanted to show her how to search for Him during difficult times. How to seek His will in all things so that she could have victory in her everyday life. He wanted to show her what real joy was, not just superficial happiness from pleasant, temporary circumstances.

When things are going smoothly, that's not necessarily true peace. True peace is knowing that God is with you, leading you, guiding you, and speaking to you during hard times.

JESUS, I'M THANKFUL I CAN FIND YOU IN EVERY HARDSHIP. I TRUST YOU WILL GIVE ME JOY IN YOUR PRESENCE!

EVERYTHING WE NEED

His divine power has given us everything we need for a godly life through our knowledge of him who called us by his own glory and goodness.

2 PETER 1:3 NIV

Barbara was a sweet elderly woman whom we met at church. She loved God with her whole heart and lived to serve Him. She became very dear to our family and taught us a lot about God. She carried on a conversation with Jesus constantly. She knew God's voice and shared with others how to hear Him too.

We didn't know it at the time, but it was her last mission on earth to share 2 Peter 1:3 with our family. We had been going through a desperately hard time, and Barbara had been praying for us daily. She brought this verse to our home along with a gift. She said that God told her to share it with us.

The very next day she fell and went to the hospital. She passed away the following week. This verse has been a constant in our family since then. We don't fight our battles in our own strength anymore. God's divine power gives us everything we need.

GOD, YOU ARE WITH ME. I KNOW I CAN FACE ANYTHING THIS WORLD THROWS AT ME BECAUSE OF YOUR DIVINE POWER ALIVE AND AT WORK IN ME!

LOVE AND LIFE

This is how God showed his love among us: He sent his one and only Son into the world that we might live through him. This is love: not that we loved God, but that he loved us and sent his Son as an atoning sacrifice for our sins. Dear friends, since God so loved us, we also ought to love one another.

1 JOHN 4:9–11 NIV

God loves you so much that He sent Jesus to die for you. And Jesus came for you so that you might come alive through Him.

In Luke 4:18–19 (NIV), Jesus said this: "The Spirit of the Lord is on me, because he has anointed me to proclaim good news to the poor. He has sent me to proclaim freedom for the prisoners and recovery of sight for the blind, to set the oppressed free, to proclaim the year of the Lord's favor."

These words from Jesus are for you! Jesus came to bring you healing and freedom from sin and death. He also came to bring you abundant life through Him that starts right now (John 10:10).

Life can be hard, but you are never alone. Jesus is with you, carrying your burdens and breathing new life into you in each moment.

JESUS, BREATHE NEW LIFE
INTO ME AS I FOLLOW YOU.

THE ONLY TRUE GOD

And we know that the Son of God has come, and he has given us understanding so that we can know the true God. And now we live in fellowship with the true God because we live in fellowship with his Son, Jesus Christ. He is the only true God, and he is eternal life.

1 JOHN 5:20 NLT

Signs of God are everywhere. Miracles are everywhere. Romans 1:20 (NIV) says, "For since the creation of the world God's invisible qualities—his eternal power and divine nature—have been clearly seen, being understood from what has been made, so that people are without excuse."

Jesus Christ is the one true God (John 1:1–5; Isaiah 9:6; John 10:30). He proved it by coming back to life after He was put to death. Everything He ever said was and is true. Isaiah 42:5–6 (NLT) says, "God, the LORD, created the heavens and stretched them out. He created the earth and everything in it. He gives breath to everyone, life to everyone who walks the earth. And it is he who says, 'I, the LORD, have called you to demonstrate my righteousness. I will take you by the hand and guard you.'"

JESUS, MY ONE TRUE GOD, I'M AMAZED THAT YOU WANT TO TAKE ME BY THE HAND AND GUIDE ME FOREVER. THANK YOU FOR GIVING ME ETERNAL LIFE!

PRAYERS AND PLANS

This is the confidence we have in approaching God:
that if we ask anything according to his will, he hears us.
And if we know that he hears us—whatever we ask—
we know that we have what we asked of him.

1 JOHN 5:14–15 NIV

God has a plan and purpose for your life. You are not an accident. You are here at this time in history and in the home that you're in with the people you love for a reason.

Acts 17:26–27 (NIV) says, "From one man he made all the nations, that they should inhabit the whole earth; and he marked out their appointed times in history and the boundaries of their lands. God did this so that they would seek him and perhaps reach out for him and find him, though he is not far from any one of us."

Isn't that amazing to think about? And if God has special plans and purposes for us, then when we ask something of God according to His will, He says, "Yes!" Second Corinthians 1:20 (NIV) says, "For no matter how many promises God has made, they are 'Yes' in Christ. And so through him the 'Amen' is spoken by us to the glory of God."

LORD, I TRUST THAT YOUR PLANS FOR ME ARE GOOD. I'M SO THANKFUL THAT YOU HEAR MY PRAYERS!

A GOOD DAD

There is no fear in love. But perfect love drives out fear, because fear has to do with punishment. The one who fears is not made perfect in love. We love because he first loved us.

1 JOHN 4:18–19 NIV

The biggest blessing in your life is that you have access to God. You can always approach Him without fear because He sees you through the love and sacrifice of Jesus. Jesus made a way once and for all. So, God is not angry with you. A person who is afraid of God's punishment doesn't understand who they are in Christ. He is a good Father, longing to hold you and love you well all the days of your life.

You don't have to work harder or be a better Christian to earn God's love. When you begin to believe who you are in Christ, it changes everything. You start living differently. You realize how deeply loved you are, and it sets you free. Remember this: As God pours His love and His Spirit into your life, His blessings spill over into the lives of those around you.

THANK YOU, FATHER, THAT I'M ABLE TO COME TO YOU WITHOUT FEAR BECAUSE OF JESUS. YOU ARE A GOOD DAD!

FEAR HAS TO LEAVE IN JESUS' NAME

You, dear children, are from God and have overcome them, because the one who is in you is greater than the one who is in the world.

1 JOHN 4:4 NIV

Is there a fear you struggle with on a regular basis? Let's deal with it today.

The Bible tells us this in Philippians 2:10 (NIV): "At the name of Jesus every knee should bow, in heaven and on earth and under the earth." Jesus is always bigger than anything you fear.

If you are in the middle of a situation that is causing you to be afraid, sometimes simply saying the name of Jesus in faith is the best prayer you can pray.

When you call on Jesus' name, you're asking Him to take your fears and fill you with His love and peace instead. The darkness has to leave when Jesus enters. Memorizing 1 John 4:4 and asking the Holy Spirit to bring it to your mind when you need it is powerful. When you are afraid, tell fear to leave in Jesus' name and declare this out loud: "Greater is He that is in me, than he that is in the world!"

JESUS, I TRUST THAT THERE IS POWER IN YOUR NAME. THANK YOU FOR RESCUING ME FROM FEAR.

CHILDREN OF GOD

See what great love the Father has lavished on us, that we should be called children of God! And that is what we are!

1 JOHN 3:1 NIV

Remember that God is a good dad—the very best. You may struggle with the way you were parented, but God parents perfectly. He always welcomes you with love and grace, even when you've made a mistake. He lavishes you with His love because you're His child. His correction is clear and kind. His discipline is loving and hope filled. He doesn't shame you.

The Bible tells us in Romans 2:4 that it is God's loving-kindness that brings us to repentance. Hebrews 12:8–10 (MSG) helps us understand this better: "Only irresponsible parents leave children to fend for themselves. Would you prefer an irresponsible God? We respect our own parents for training and not spoiling us, so why not embrace God's training so we can truly live? While we were children, our parents did what seemed best to them. But God is doing what is best for us, training us to live God's holy best."

God cares about the choices you make and the struggles you face. He trains you to live your best life in Christ.

HEAVENLY FATHER, I'M THANKFUL THAT I'M YOUR CHILD! I TRUST THAT YOU ARE TRAINING ME TO BE MORE LIKE YOU.

WHILE WE WERE SINNERS

God clearly shows and proves His own love for us,
by the fact that while we were still sinners, Christ died for us.
ROMANS 5:8 AMP

Beloved daughter of God, you can do nothing to earn God's love for you. Before the creation of the world, God had His heart set on you. He knows everything you've ever done and everything you ever will do. And still, He loves you perfectly! You are loved, valued, and cherished by God simply because you're His child.

When you mess up, God loves you. When you succeed, God loves you. When you fail, God loves you. You cannot disappoint God. Thinking that God is disappointed in you is a form of unbelief. Disappointment has to do with expectation. Would God ever be surprised by something you do? Nope. Because He already knows everything, from beginning to end.

God looks on you and smiles because He sees you through the love and sacrifice of Jesus Christ.

When you mess up, you can go boldly to the throne of grace and find mercy (Hebrews 4:16) and forgiveness from the one who loves you and has great plans for your life.

I'M SO AMAZED AT YOUR AMAZING GRACE AND LOVE FOR ME, FATHER! THANK YOU FOR SENDING JESUS TO MAKE A WAY FOR ME TO BE IN YOUR PRESENCE FOREVER.

STRUGGLING WITH SERVICE

We are confident of all this because of our great trust in God through Christ. It is not that we think we are qualified to do anything on our own. Our qualification comes from God.

2 CORINTHIANS 3:4–5 NLT

Have you ever questioned your ability to serve God well? Maybe you think you're not talented enough, not smart enough, not outgoing enough, not (fill in the blank) enough.

The truth is that when we're Christ followers, Jesus will cover our weaknesses with His strength. Where we come up short, He will provide. He will make us "enough" to do His work!

First Peter 4:10 (NLT) tells us, "God has given each of you a gift from his great variety of spiritual gifts. Use them well to serve one another."

As a child of God, you've been given gifts to serve Him. Sitting in the pew and racing out before the "amen" isn't going to cut it. But you don't have to worry about what you're going to do or how—not when you invite Jesus to be your strength and guide.

Whatever God is calling you to do, He'll provide the strength and energy and ability to get it done.

LORD, I'M STRUGGLING WITH WHAT I'M SUPPOSED TO DO AND HOW. PLEASE SHOW ME THE WAY FORWARD. FILL ME WITH YOUR STRENGTH AND ABILITY TO DO WHATEVER YOU ASK.

EXPERIENCE JESUS

For God, who said, "Let there be light in the darkness," has made this light shine in our hearts so we could know the glory of God that is seen in the face of Jesus Christ.

2 CORINTHIANS 4:6 NLT

There are believers who know a whole lot about Jesus but have never experienced Him. These people are often the ones who run out of their own strength. They've been puffed up with knowledge but never built up and strengthened by the love of God (1 Corinthians 8:1). They "deconstruct" because their faith is built on knowledge rather than experience.

How about you? Have you allowed the light of Jesus to shine in your heart? Have you rested in His presence, allowing Him to fill you with love and strength?

Psalm 84:11 (NLT) says, "For the LORD God is our sun and our shield. He gives us grace and glory. The LORD will withhold no good thing from those who do what is right."

Sit in God's presence. Let Him be your sun and shield. Let Him love you. This intimate experience fills you with the strength you need to live the life God has for you—a full and abundant life (John 10:10).

LORD, I'M NEW AT THIS. BE MY TEACHER AS I LEARN TO SIT IN YOUR PRESENCE AND BE FILLED WITH YOUR LOVE BEFORE I START "DOING."

ARMED AND READY

Therefore put on the full armor of God, so that when the day of evil comes, you may be able to stand your ground, and after you have done everything, to stand.

EPHESIANS 6:13 NIV

As a child of God, you are deeply loved and valued. God is a good Father, and He prepares His children well. He has given you special armor to wear when you are fighting life's battles.

Here's what's included in your armor (see Ephesians 6:10–17):

- belt of truth
- breastplate of righteousness
- shoes ready to carry the gospel of peace
- shield of faith
- helmet of salvation
- sword of the Spirit

The belt of truth keeps everything in the right place. When you know the truth about who God is and who He says you are, you can make it through any battle. Add your breastplate of righteousness, the shoes of the gospel of peace, the shield of faith to extinguish the enemy's flaming arrows, the helmet of salvation, and then the sword of the Spirit, which is God's Word. With all of this, you are armed and ready for whatever life throws your way!

LORD, THANKS FOR PREPARING ME FOR LIFE'S BATTLES. I'M THANKFUL I DON'T FIGHT IN MY OWN STRENGTH!

THE COST OF FOLLOWING JESUS

After proclaiming the Message in Derbe and establishing a strong core of disciples, they retraced their steps to Lystra, then Iconium, and then Antioch, putting grit in the lives of the disciples, urging them to stick with what they had begun to believe and not quit, making it clear to them that it wouldn't be easy: "Anyone signing up for the kingdom of God has to go through plenty of hard times."

ACTS 14:21–22 MSG

Paul and Barnabas were sharing the gospel and preaching in cities all around Asia, as noted in the book of Acts. The Bible says they spoke boldly for Jesus, but the people were divided in their support and acceptance of the message. One group of people even plotted to stone them.

Obeying God in this fallen world is not going to be easy. Hard times and trials will come our way often, but don't lose heart!

Charles Spurgeon said: "So surely as the stars are fashioned by His hands, and their orbits fixed by Him, so surely are our trials allotted to us: He has ordained their season and their place, their intensity and the effect they shall have upon us."

LORD, I KNOW I CAN TRUST YOU WITH MY LIFE. I'M BEGINNING TO UNDERSTAND THAT YOU ALONE PROVIDE THE STRENGTH I NEED FOR THE STRUGGLES I FACE.

IN IT TOGETHER

Don't be intimidated in any way by your enemies. . . .
We are in this struggle together. You have seen my struggle in the past, and you know that I am still in the midst of it.

PHILIPPIANS 1:28, 30 NLT

Intimidating people can be a regular source of our struggles. The early church experienced this in dangerous ways. In Philippians 1, Paul encouraged the believers to remember that they were not alone. Christians everywhere were facing the same kind of struggles.

Philippians 1:6 (NLT) says, "I am certain that God, who began the good work within you, will continue his work until it is finally finished on the day when Christ Jesus returns."

If you're in a situation where you feel intimidated and you're in need of courage and strength, remember that God can move things and change things in your favor in ways far beyond your imagination. Trust His love and care for you! And remember you're never alone. Christians around the world are in the struggle with you. Pray for them too.

LORD GOD, I'M LEARNING TO TRUST YOU MORE, AND IT IS SO EXCITING. YOU CAN DO MORE THAN I EVER THOUGHT POSSIBLE. PLEASE GIVE ME STRENGTH AND COURAGE TO DO WHAT YOU ASK. I TRUST THAT YOU'LL HANDLE THE OUTCOME.

GOD'S LOVE SONG

I will sing of your strength, in the morning I will sing of your love; for you are my fortress, my refuge in times of trouble.

PSALM 59:16 NIV

Ever feel like your mind is a muddle? Like the world is spinning out of your control and you need a breather?

Stop right now. Breathe deeply. Spend some time with God in creation and clear your head. Check out these scriptures:

- "The heavens declare the glory of God; the skies proclaim the work of his hands" (Psalm 19:1 NIV).
- "The birds nest beside the streams and sing among the branches of the trees. You send rain on the mountains from your heavenly home, and you fill the earth with the fruit of your labor" (Psalm 104:12–13 NLT).
- "Our help is from the LORD, who made heaven and earth" (Psalm 124:8 NLT).

Head outside and take a look at the beautiful world around you. Marvel at the wonders God created, the miracle of birds that sing, the glorious sky, and the weather that is forever changing. Creation is bursting with joy all around you, singing God's love song to you.

LORD, I'M SO THANKFUL THAT YOU SPEAK TO ME THROUGH YOUR CREATION. HELP ME TO NOTICE YOUR LOVE SONGS IN CREATION. THANK YOU FOR FILLING ME WITH JOY IN YOUR PRESENCE TODAY!

PASS IT ON

Know therefore that the LORD your God is God; he is the faithful God, keeping his covenant of love to a thousand generations of those who love him and keep his commandments.

DEUTERONOMY 7:9 NIV

Special protection is available to you when you love God and follow His ways. The Bible says it extends to generation after generation. This doesn't mean that you and your children won't have problems to overcome if you love God. But it does mean that God is with you in the struggles, always working everything out for your good and His glory (Romans 8:28), turning every pain and heartache into something beautiful (Ecclesiastes 3:11).

Imagine watching a movie where nothing dangerous or adventurous ever happened. Sounds like a documentary on the history of boredom! Who wants that kind of life? God wants us to live an abundant and full life of adventure in Christ. Problems and struggles will come, but you can also experience an abundance of God's presence and joy in the midst of those struggles.

Was your faith in Christ passed down in your family? Be thankful! Who will *you* pass it on to? A rich heritage of faith and love is an extraordinary gift!

LORD, HELP ME TO LOVE WELL AND PASS MY FAITH ON TO THE NEXT GENERATION.

RESTORATION

If we confess our sins, he is faithful and just and will forgive us our sins and purify us from all unrighteousness.

1 John 1:9 NIV

We all mess up. It's part of being human. Sometimes you might be tempted to hide from God when you sin. That's what Adam and Eve did, right? But God wants you to come to Him instead. Talk to Him about it. Run into His arms and trust Him to be faithful to you.

The Amplified Bible explains that God "will forgive our sins and cleanse us continually from all unrighteousness [our wrongdoing, everything not in conformity with His will and purpose]."

There is something very powerful about coming to God and confessing your sins to Him. He wants to cleanse you "continually." He wants to help you through your situation and give you peace. He wants to remind you of who you really are—His child!

Jesus already paid the price for your sin—once and for all on the cross. And so, your salvation is secure. And when you come to Him after you've messed up, you get to clear the air and be restored. Your relationship with God grows deeper and stronger.

LORD, THANK YOU FOR YOUR FAITHFULNESS! I COME TO YOU WITH ALL MY SIN AND ASK THAT YOU WOULD CHANGE ME AND RESTORE OUR RELATIONSHIP.

HOLD NOTHING BACK WITH GOD

But You, O Lord, are a God [who protects and is] merciful and gracious, slow to anger and abounding in lovingkindness and truth.

PSALM 86:15 AMP

King David had many struggles. He knew what it was like to be bullied. Take a look at this paraphrase from *The Message*: "A gang of thugs is after me—and they don't care a thing about you. But you, O God, are both tender and kind, not easily angered, immense in love, and you never, never quit. So look me in the eye and show kindness, give your servant the strength to go on, save your dear, dear child! Make a show of how much you love me so the bullies who hate me will stand there slack-jawed, as you, GOD, gently and powerfully put me back on my feet" (Psalm 86:14–17).

David had a very personal and emotional relationship with God. He shared his deepest thoughts and feelings with God, holding nothing back. Friend, God wants that same kind of relationship with you!

If you're struggling with people, bring it to God. Let Him love you and lead you. Watch as He "gently and powerfully" puts you back on your feet.

THANK YOU FOR YOUR KINDNESS TO ME, LORD. THANK YOU FOR GIVING ME STRENGTH AS I BRING MY STRUGGLES WITH PEOPLE TO YOU.

DON'T FAKE IT

Don't just pretend to love others. Really love them. Hate what is wrong. Hold tightly to what is good. Love each other with genuine affection, and take delight in honoring each other.

Romans 12:9–10 NLT

When you're dealing with difficult people, allow God to fill you up with His love for them. You don't have to exhaust yourself *trying* to be nice to someone who is hard to love. Remember, people can tell when you're faking it. Pray for them instead. And God will help you respond to them with His love. He will give you His strength to do the things He's calling you to do.

Romans 12 goes on to talk about right and wrong, good and evil. God wants you to turn away and run from evil and instead to hold tightly to His truth and to what is good. The chapter concludes by saying, "Don't let evil conquer you, but conquer evil by doing good" (verse 21 NLT).

This is all very timely encouragement from God's Word for the culture we live in! It can be summed up like this: Love God, love others, run from evil, and hang on to the truth of scripture!

LORD, I'M DEALING WITH DIFFICULT PEOPLE. PLEASE GIVE ME YOUR LOVE FOR THEM.

JESUS' PRAYER FOR BELIEVERS

"Now I am departing from the world; they are staying in this world, but I am coming to you. Holy Father, you have given me your name; now protect them by the power of your name so that they will be united just as we are."

JOHN 17:11 NLT

Did you know that Jesus was praying for you? In John 17, the Bible records several long prayers that Jesus prayed for Himself, for His disciples, and for future believers—you!

Jesus prayed to His Father that there would be unity among believers so that "the world will know that you sent me and have loved them even as you have loved me" (verse 23 NIV).

Jesus also prayed that we would be protected by the power of God's name. Proverbs 18:10 (NLT) says, "The name of the LORD is a strong fortress; the godly run to him and are safe."

Psalm 3:5 (NLT) says, "I lay down and slept, yet I woke up in safety, for the LORD was watching over me."

God is watching over you and protecting you. You don't have to fear a single thing.

LORD, I PRAY FOR UNITY AMONG BELIEVERS. HELP ME TO LOVE PEOPLE LIKE YOU DO. THANK YOU FOR PROTECTING ME BY THE POWER OF YOUR NAME.

VIEW TROUBLE AS TRAINING

We can rejoice, too, when we run into problems and trials, for we know that they help us develop endurance. And endurance develops strength of character, and character strengthens our confident hope of salvation.

ROMANS 5:3–4 NLT

What if you found out that the surgeon assigned to you or a family member got poor grades in school and skipped over several difficult and important trainings? Would you want that person doing surgery on you or someone you love? Probably not. Or what about a brand-new pilot who had never flown a plane with people in it before? Would you want to fly over the ocean with that guy in charge? No thanks.

Training is extremely important. God trains us through the struggles we go through in life. Is it difficult for you to see the problems and trials you face in this life as training? Perhaps, but through it all, God is guiding you to be the person He created you to be. As you learn under His instruction, you'll develop endurance, character, and hope!

With this perspective, you can rejoice and have peace in Christ when trouble comes, because you know that God is with you in the struggles. And He will use everything that happens for your good (Romans 8:28).

LORD, THANK YOU FOR GIVING ME A NEW PERSPECTIVE ABOUT THE STRUGGLES I FACE.

WE HAVE GOD'S SPIRIT

"In the last days, God says, I will pour out my Spirit on all people. Your sons and daughters will prophesy, your young men will see visions, your old men will dream dreams."

ACTS 2:17 NIV

God knew we couldn't figure out life on our own. He knew we would need a helper to teach us and lead us. So, He sent His very own Spirit to live and grow inside of us. This is very important to remember!

Look at what *The Message* says: "Spiritually alive, we have access to everything God's Spirit is doing. . . . Isaiah's question, 'Is there anyone around who knows God's Spirit, anyone who knows what he is doing?' has been answered: Christ knows, and we have Christ's Spirit" (1 Corinthians 2:15–16).

When we have the Spirit of Jesus alive in us, we are being transformed. God's Word is brought to life in us, and we are taught right and wrong. Because God loves you so much, He sent His Spirit to come alive in you. If you've accepted Jesus Christ as your Lord and Savior, His Spirit is alive and at work in you this very moment!

I COULDN'T DO LIFE WITHOUT YOUR SPIRIT, LORD! THANK YOU FOR HELPING ME LIVE THE CHRISTIAN LIFE THROUGH YOUR STRENGTH AND POWER.

MY GOOD SHEPHERD

"My sheep listen to my voice; I know them, and they follow me. I give them eternal life, and they shall never perish; no one will snatch them out of my hand. My Father, who has given them to me, is greater than all; no one can snatch them out of my Father's hand."

JOHN 10:27–29 NIV

There are online videos that show modern-day shepherds (yes, there still are some!) with several herds of sheep together. One shepherd moves away from the large herd and calls his own sheep to him. His flock of sheep know his voice and move as a group toward his voice. The remaining sheep go toward the call of their own shepherd. It's really amazing to watch!

In John 10:11 (AMPC), Jesus says, "I am the Good Shepherd. The Good Shepherd risks and lays down His [own] life for the sheep." Our shepherd gave His very life for us! And He wants us to know His voice.

Spend time with Jesus in His Word. Be still in His presence and let Him speak to you. Ask Him to be your good and gentle shepherd.

JESUS, YOU ARE MY GOOD SHEPHERD. OPEN MYEARS TO HEAR YOUR VOICE. THANK YOU FOR YOUR GENTLE CARE.

GOD'S ECONOMY

"For all the animals of the forest are mine,
and I own the cattle on a thousand hills."
PSALM 50:10 NLT

Things have a miraculous way of working out in God's economy. Remember Romans 8:28? God is at work. He owns the cattle on a thousand hills. What does that mean? God has every resource at His disposal. Everything is His! He can do anything, and He promises to meet your every need.

When our daughter had surgery in a new town after we moved across the country, God arranged for one of our only friends in the area to be working at the hospital that day. We had to arrive before 6:00 a.m. for prep. She was just getting off her shift at that time, and she met us at the doors, wheeled us to the place we needed to go in a hospital where we didn't know our way around, and prayed over our daughter and for the surgeon before she left. We couldn't have arranged all that if we'd tried!

Be encouraged that every decision and plan isn't all on your shoulders. It's not all up to you. God sees you and will provide for all your needs.

LORD, I'M SO THANKFUL THAT YOU PROMISE TO MEET ALL MY NEEDS. HELP ME TRUST YOU IN THIS!

REFUEL

I hear the tumult of the raging seas as your waves and surging tides sweep over me. But each day the Lord pours his unfailing love upon me, and through each night I sing his songs, praying to God who gives me life.

Psalm 42:7–8 NLT

God is always speaking to you. Are you listening? He cares about every need and every thought that weighs heavily on your heart. He wants to speak to you about every emotion and circumstance.

The writer of Psalm 42 sings of raging seas and discouragement. He is clearly struggling. But he remembers that God pours out His unfailing love on His children every day and that he can worship and talk to God throughout every moment. Day by day and night by night he is refueled with God's strength and love.

God is present in your circumstances. He is up to something good, no matter what things look and feel like right now. You have a special place in God's heart, and He wants you to bring every thought to Him. He is speaking in the wind and rain, in His Word, through songs, through people, and so much more.

LORD GOD, I NEED A REFILLING OF YOUR LOVE AND STRENGTH IN MY LIFE. HELP ME TO LISTEN AS YOU SPEAK TRUTH TO ME. OPEN MY EARS TO HEAR FROM YOU, LORD.

FEELING THE JOY

Satisfy us in the morning with your unfailing love,
that we may sing for joy and be glad all our days.
PSALM 90:14 NIV

Your feelings and your attitude are important to God. And guess what? Jesus promises to fill you with His joy when you spend time with Him.

Check out these verses from the Bible:

- "You make known to me the path of life; you will fill me with joy in your presence" (Psalm 16:11 NIV).
- "I am coming to you now, but I say these things while I am still in the world, so that they may have the full measure of my joy within them" (John 17:13 NIV).
- "May the God of hope fill you with all joy and peace as you trust in him, so that you may overflow with hope by the power of the Holy Spirit" (Romans 15:13 NIV).

Spend time with Jesus, and He'll fill you with joy. He is with you in this very moment. If you're having trouble feeling joy in your life, get alone somewhere and talk to God. Tell Him exactly how you feel, and then let Him help.

JESUS, I'M THANKFUL FOR YOUR PROMISE OF JOY AS I SPEND TIME WITH YOU. HELP ME KNOW AND EXPERIENCE YOUR TRUE JOY AND PEACE THROUGH THE POWER OF YOUR SPIRIT.

UNSEEN BATTLE

"Don't be afraid," the prophet answered. "Those who are with us are more than those who are with them."

2 KINGS 6:16 NIV

The book of 2 Kings has an amazing account of the prophet Elisha providing the king of Israel with information about the movements of the Aramean army who fought against Israel. One night the Aramean king went after Elisha to capture him with chariots and soldiers.

Elisha's servant got up early the next morning to see that they were surrounded by the enemy. He was alarmed. But Elisha told him not to be afraid. He knew God would take care of them. Elisha asked God to open the servant's eyes to see into the spiritual realm. Second Kings 6:17 (NIV) says, "Elisha prayed, 'Open his eyes, LORD, so that he may see.' Then the LORD opened the servant's eyes, and he looked and saw the hills full of horses and chariots of fire all around Elisha."

The servant saw that he and Elisha were protected by unseen forces. God had sent His angels and a heavenly army to protect them. And friend, the God of Elisha is your God too. He is the God of miracles who will shelter and protect you from evil as you rest in Him.

WOW, GOD! YOU ARE AMAZING!
HELP ME TRUST THAT YOU CAN PROTECT
ME JUST LIKE YOU PROTECTED ELISHA!

SAFE IN HIS ARMS

Whoever dwells in the shelter of the Most High will rest in the shadow of the Almighty. I will say of the LORD, "He is my refuge and my fortress, my God, in whom I trust."

PSALM 91:1–2 NIV

If you dwell in Christ, you can rest in Him. When you go after things in your own strength, you can't keep up. But trusting in Christ and seeking His strength allows you to rest in peace because you know He is fighting your battles.

Imagine a mom who wants her timid toddler to know that it is safe to swing on the swing set. The mom places her toddler in her lap and gets on the swing. Before you know it, the toddler is giggling and then releasing a full-on belly laugh! The toddler is safe and full of joy! Now he's ready to try it by himself.

Imagine Jesus doing that with you. You are safe in His arms. He's the wisest and most perfect parent. You can trust that whatever happens is for your good. Nothing coming after you is bigger than our God! You can find joy even in the struggles. He's got you.

LORD, THANK YOU FOR PARENTING ME PERFECTLY. I KNOW I AM SAFE IN YOUR ARMS.

STRENGTH THAT NEVER FAILS

Be strong in the Lord [draw your strength from Him and be empowered through your union with Him] and in the power of His [boundless] might.

EPHESIANS 6:10 AMP

As a young Irish woman, Amy Carmichael began hearing from God and knew that He had a special plan for her life despite her poor health. God led her to India to an area where young girls were given away to the temple gods. God used Amy to rescue many of them.

Carmichael is often credited with saying, "It is great to be faced with the impossible, for nothing is impossible if one is meant to do it. Wisdom will be given, and strength. When the Lord leads, He always strengthens."

God showed His great love for Amy and for all the young girls she rescued by God giving her His strength, even when she was weak. Amy was bedridden for the final years of her life. During that time of great pain, she continued to encourage others by writing them letters. Here is an excerpt she wrote to a friend: "Pain is never easy to bear, and you have had so much of it. But help comes, doesn't it? Strength for the day, strength for the minute. And it will never fail us if only we look up."

LORD, PLEASE GIVE ME THE STRENGTH TO ENCOURAGE OTHERS EVEN WHEN I'M STRUGGLING.

PSALM 139

You know what I am going to say even before I say it, Lord. You go before me and follow me. You place your hand of blessing on my head.

Psalm 139:4–5 NLT

Psalm 139 begins, "O Lord, you have searched me [thoroughly] and have known me. You know when I sit down and when I rise up [my entire life, everything I do]; You understand my thought from afar. You scrutinize my path and my lying down, and You are intimately acquainted with all my ways" (verses 1–3 AMP).

Verses 5 and 6 (NLT) say, "You go before me and follow me. You place your hand of blessing on my head. Such knowledge is too wonderful for me, too great for me to understand!"

You are fully known and valued by your Father in heaven. He cherishes you and delights in you. Whenever you are feeling far from God, open your Bible to Psalm 139. Read it slowly and allow God's Word to fill you with His love and strength.

THANK YOU FOR THE BEAUTIFUL TRUTHS I FIND IN YOUR WORD, FATHER GOD! I'M SO GRATEFUL THAT YOU SEE ME AND LOVE ME LIKE YOU DO.

HOPE DURING PERSECUTION

You, however, know all about my teaching, my way of life, my purpose, faith, patience, love, endurance, persecutions, sufferings. . .the persecutions I endured. Yet the Lord rescued me from all of them. In fact, everyone who wants to live a godly life in Christ Jesus will be persecuted.

2 TIMOTHY 3:10–12 NIV

Adoniram Judson was a missionary to Burma in Southeast Asia during the 1800s. As a foreign missionary and Bible translator, he faced many difficulties. His children died, his wife died at a young age, and he was imprisoned. He went through an extended depression and isolation. But during that time, he kept reading and praying. About all his heartache, he said this: "If I had not felt certain that every additional trial was ordered by infinite love and mercy, I could not have survived my accumulated sufferings."*

Matthew 5:10 (AMP) gives us great hope: "Blessed [comforted by inner peace and God's love] are those who are persecuted for doing that which is morally right, for theirs is the kingdom of heaven [both now and forever]."

In all your struggles and persecutions, remember that God Himself will give you the strength to overcome.

**Giants of the Missionary Trail* (Chicago: Scripture Press Foundation, 1954), 73.

THANK YOU FOR THE GREAT HOPE I FIND IN YOUR WORD, LORD JESUS! I TRUST THAT YOUR INFINITE LOVE AND MERCY ARE AT WORK IN ALL MY CIRCUMSTANCES.

HAGAR'S STORY

Then she called the name of the LORD who spoke to her, "You are God Who Sees"; for she said, "Have I not even here [in the wilderness] remained alive after seeing Him [who sees me with understanding and compassion]?"

GENESIS 16:13 AMP

In the Bible, a young Egyptian girl named Hagar was a servant of Abram's wife, Sarai. Sadly, Sarai thought God needed help delivering on some of His promises, and so she used and abused Hagar in the process.

Hagar was so upset that she ran away from Abram and Sarai. In Genesis 16, we see that an angel of the Lord was sent to Hagar to comfort her and give her hope and direction. He found her alone in the desert. Hagar was amazed that God cared about her—an Egyptian servant girl! Because of this, she called God the "God Who Sees," and her story was recorded in scripture.

Just as with Hagar, God cares about your struggles and your thoughts. He knows your heart, and He knows why you do the things you do. God sees you with understanding and compassion. He cares about your hopes and dreams. He knows exactly what you need.

I'M AMAZED THAT YOU KNOW ME AND LOVE ME SO PERSONALLY, FATHER GOD!

STRUGGLING WITH INSECURITY

Even before he made the world, God loved us and chose us in Christ to be holy and without fault in his eyes. God decided in advance to adopt us into his own family by bringing us to himself through Jesus Christ. This is what he wanted to do, and it gave him great pleasure.

EPHESIANS 1:4–5 NLT

Do you sometimes worry about what other people think of you? Do you dress for the approval of others? Panic a little when someone doesn't text you back? These are signs that you may have an insecurity problem.

Insecurity is rooted in fear, and it's something Jesus has given you authority over. He wants to help you overcome insecurity for good. How can you do this?

First, the Bible says to submit yourself to God, to resist the devil and he will flee from you (James 4:7). Kick those insecure and discouraging thoughts to the curb. Tell them to get lost in the name and authority of Jesus.

Then, replace those negative thoughts with truth from God's Word. Look up scriptures, write them down, and hang them up where you'll see them daily. The Holy Spirit will help you memorize them. Speak them out loud!

LORD, THANKS FOR LOVING ME SO MUCH THAT YOU GAVE ME TOOLS TO OVERCOME INSECURITY!

LOVE COMES FROM GOD

Dear friends, let us love one another, for love comes from God. Everyone who loves has been born of God and knows God. Whoever does not love does not know God, because God is love.

1 JOHN 4:7–8 NIV

God is love, and love comes from Him. We all know something about real love. Thankfully, God has given us other people to love and who love us in return. We also know that love isn't just a feeling—it's a choice to care for others and put their needs above our own.

But if we're honest, there are people in our lives who are difficult to love. What do we do about them?

Remember, love comes from God. You don't have to pretend to love someone with love you don't have. People see right through any kind of fakeness anyhow. When you are struggling to love someone else, ask God to give you His love for that person. Start praying for them. Sometimes love looks like setting boundaries or having a direct conversation with a difficult person. God will give you strength and wisdom for that.

God is the source of love, and He will supply all you need to share His love with others, even the unlovable.

LORD, I'M ASKING FOR STRENGTH AND WISDOM TO LOVE THE UNLOVABLE PEOPLE IN MY LIFE.

LIFE-CHANGING WORD

This is how God showed his love among us: He sent his one and only Son into the world that we might live through him. This is love: not that we loved God, but that he loved us and sent his Son as an atoning sacrifice for our sins.

1 JOHN 4:9–10 NIV

One of my friends was struggling. She had spent most of her teenage years trying to do the right thing and love God. But hard things kept happening, and she lost her way. She still believed God was real; she just believed that He was disappointed in her.

My friend had a hard time feeling like God (or anyone else, for that matter) loved her at all. And she certainly didn't have loving feelings toward God. In fact, she didn't have any feelings at all. Is numb a feeling? Then that's what she was.

One day she came across this verse in her Bible and the words jumped out at her: "This is love: not that we loved God, but that he loved us." The Holy Spirit brought those words to life in her heart, and she began to understand that nothing she had ever done or ever could do would change God's love for her.

Those words changed her life!

LORD, I'M SO THANKFUL THAT YOUR WORD STILL HAS THE POWER TO CHANGE LIVES TODAY!

TELL YOURSELF THE TRUTH

For the Spirit God gave us does not make us timid,
but gives us power, love and self-discipline.
2 TIMOTHY 1:7 NIV

The Amplified Bible explains 2 Timothy 1:7 this way: "For God did not give us a spirit of timidity or cowardice or fear, but [He has given us a spirit] of power and of love and of sound judgment and personal discipline [abilities that result in a calm, well-balanced mind and self-control]."

This scripture can be especially helpful when you're struggling with fear or brain fog, or feeling like you're going crazy. Maybe the problems are piling on and you can't even think straight. This is a verse you need to set your mind on. Write it down. Keep it close. Say it out loud when the enemy's lies are coming for you.

Telling yourself the truth is vital. Do not align with the enemy's lies. Truth from God's Word counteracts what the enemy is trying to do to you. God's Spirit gives you power, love, and a sound mind that results in self-control.

LORD, I AGREE WITH THE TRUTH OF YOUR WORD. YOU'VE GIVEN ME A SOUND MIND, AND I TRUST THAT YOU WILL STRENGTHEN ME TO DO WHAT YOU'VE CALLED ME TO DO.

MY SHIELD OF LOVE

For you bless the godly, O Lord;
you surround them with your shield of love.
PSALM 5:12 NLT

King David wrote Psalm 5 as a prayer to God concerning his enemies. Because David's enemies were lying about him, his heart was hurting, and so he would go to God each day in prayer, asking God to shield and protect him from the lies.

When someone is spreading rumors about you, it hurts. The enemy is prowling, trying to get you to believe his lies and doubt God. Resist and run into God's arms instead. Let Him be your shield of love in those situations.

David wrote in Psalm 5:2–3 (NLT), "Listen to my cry for help, my King and my God, for I pray to no one but you. Listen to my voice in the morning, LORD. Each morning I bring my requests to you and wait expectantly." David knew that God would help. Not only can God protect our hearts and heal us from every hurt, but He is also the strongest force there ever was and ever will be! He is able to silence any lie and thwart any weapon that comes against His beloved children (Isaiah 54:17). Let Him love you. Let Him shield you.

LORD, PLEASE SILENCE THE LIES OF MY ENEMIES. BE MY SHIELD OF LOVE. THANK YOU FOR HEARING MY PRAYERS!

RELY ON GOD

For in Him our heart rejoices, because we trust [lean on, rely on, and are confident] in His holy name.

PSALM 33:21 AMP

If you got up yesterday and surrendered your will for God's, finding His strength in your weakness, that's great! But that doesn't mean you get a pass for today. God wants you to come to Him every day, relying on Him to meet each need you have.

He helps us sort out our wants from our needs. And for anything you *need,* God has you covered! If it's strength for your weakness, it's yours. If you need daily bread, you will find it. If it's a physical need, you can trust that God will take care of you.

Check this out: "And God is able to make all grace [every favor and earthly blessing] come in abundance to you, so that you may always [under all circumstances, regardless of the need] have complete sufficiency in everything [being completely self-sufficient in Him], and have an abundance for every good work and act of charity" (2 Corinthians 9:8 AMP).

LORD, I WANT TO RELY ON YOU FOR MY EVERY NEED. PLEASE PLANT A DEEP DESIRE IN MY HEART TO COME TO YOU EVERY DAY.

HE WILL NEVER FAIL YOU

And my God will liberally supply (fill until full) your every need according to His riches in glory in Christ Jesus.

PHILIPPIANS 4:19 AMP

George Müller, a missionary who ran an orphanage in the 1800s, learned to rely wholly upon God. He kept a journal in which he recorded all the amazing miracles of God he experienced. One such miracle was when the orphanage was completely out of food and money. He said that before school they prayed and thanked God for what He would bring them to eat.

There soon was a knock on the door from a baker who said he felt God telling him to bring bread. And then another knock from the milkman, whose cart broke down right outside the orphanage. God sent the children their breakfast. Mr. Müller learned to pray about every need, and he taught the children to do the same.

God promises to meet your every need as well. You can rely on Him fully. You don't ever have to take matters into your own hands.

George Müller said that if you walk with God and expect Him to help you, He'll never let you down.

LORD, I REPENT OF TAKING MATTERS INTO MY OWN HANDS. HELP ME LEARN TO RELY ON YOU TO MEET ALL MY NEEDS.

REMINDERS OF GOD'S LOVE

I will instruct you and teach you in the way you should go; I will counsel you [who are willing to learn] with My eye upon you.

PSALM 32:8 AMP

Here's your daily reminder that God loves you! He is close. The Bible says that He sees you. He cares about you personally, knowing the things that are on your heart and mind. Check out these scriptures that show how much God cares about you:

- "The LORD is close to the brokenhearted and saves those who are crushed in spirit" (Psalm 34:18 NIV).
- "The LORD appeared to us in the past, saying: 'I have loved you with an everlasting love; I have drawn you with unfailing kindness'" (Jeremiah 31:3 NIV).
- "Even though I am afflicted and needy, still the Lord takes thought and is mindful of me. You are my help and my rescuer. O my God, do not delay" (Psalm 40:17 AMP).
- "You keep track of all my sorrows. You have collected all my tears in your bottle. You have recorded each one in your book" (Psalm 56:8 NLT).
- "Cast all your anxiety on him because he cares for you" (1 Peter 5:7 NIV).

God cares deeply about you! Invite Him to be your teacher and counselor.

I'M SO THANKFUL FOR YOUR LOVE, LORD GOD! I AM WILLING TO LEARN FROM YOU.

NEVER FORGET

Let all that I am praise the L*ORD; with my whole heart, I will praise his holy name. Let all that I am praise the* L*ORD; may I never forget the good things he does for me.*

PSALM 103:1–2 NLT

When you go through a powerful, mountaintop experience with God, you might think you will never forget it! But when you are struggling in the valley, months or years later, you might not remember what God did for you at the top. In the brain fog of struggle, remembering won't be that easy.

If you've never started the spiritual practice of journaling, give it a try. This doesn't have to be fancy or time-consuming with special pens and flowery words. Simply write down a prayer list and notate when God answers. It's that simple.

God answers prayers, and He is always speaking. Writing down how He has answered you personally can help boost your faith in times of doubt.

Psalm 42:4 (NIV) says, "These things I remember as I pour out my soul."

As you pour out your soul to the Lord, remember what He has done for you in the past!

LORD, REMIND ME OF THE THINGS YOU HAVE DONE IN MY LIFE AND THE PRAYERS YOU HAVE ANSWERED. HELP ME TO GET IN THE HABIT OF WRITING THEM DOWN SO I NEVER FORGET.

CALM FOR THE SOUL

The L*ORD* *says, "I will rescue those who love me. I will protect those who trust in my name. When they call on me, I will answer; I will be with them in trouble. I will rescue and honor them. I will reward them with a long life and give them my salvation."*

PSALM 91:14–16 NLT

A young Christian woman began having panic attacks. She'd been through a traumatic event, and she couldn't get her brain to stop replaying the incident. During the incident, she was in great danger, but she was rescued at the last minute. She was thankful to be alive. However, she couldn't stop thinking about how close she came to death, and she was having nightmares.

She went to see a Christian trauma therapist to help her move forward in life. He pointed her to Jesus and the need of the Holy Spirit to help her take those thoughts captive. During their therapy, the counselor recommended that she read Psalm 91 before going to sleep every night. This helped calm her and reminded her of how much God cares for her. The psalm reminds us of God's help and protection in any kind of danger.

GOD, YOUR WORD IS ALIVE AND POWERFUL (HEBREWS 4:12). THANK YOU FOR CALMING MY SOUL THROUGH YOUR HOLY SCRIPTURES.

NO MORE GRUMPY DAYS

I know what it is to be in need, and I know what it is to have plenty. I have learned the secret of being content in any and every situation, whether well fed or hungry, whether living in plenty or in want. I can do all this through him who gives me strength.

PHILIPPIANS 4:12–13 NIV

The wrong side of the bed is an awful place to wake up and start your day. If you look that phrase up in the online *Oxford Dictionary* it says, "start the day in a bad mood, which continues all day long." Look out! No one wants to get in the way of *that* person! But what if that person is you?

Our mood of the day is a choice, isn't it? You may wake up sick and tired, but you *always* get to choose your attitude.

Paul had figured this out. The secret is allowing Jesus Christ to be your source of strength and happiness in every situation. Ask God to help you choose joy and thankfulness every day of your life. He loves you, and He has great plans for you—and that's something to be joyful about!

Choosing to be thankful for what you have can change a grumpy, no-good day to a day full of happiness and adventure. And the best part of it is that *you* get to make this *choice*—it's one thing you do have control over.

LORD, I NEED YOUR STRENGTH TO CHOOSE JOY, NO MATTER HOW I'M FEELING IN THE MOMENT.

ALIGN YOUR THOUGHTS WITH TRUTH

You will keep in perfect peace all who trust in you, all whose thoughts are fixed on you!

ISAIAH 26:3 NLT

The Bible talks about taking every thought captive and making it obedient to Christ (2 Corinthians 10:5). This is a very big deal if you want to have a personal relationship with God.

How do you take your thoughts captive and fix them on Jesus? You align your thoughts with God's thoughts. You fill your mind with His truth. You invite the Holy Spirit to speak to your heart, reminding you of God's truth.

Here's a helpful way to follow through on these things: Make a list of struggles or lies that regularly haunt you. Then find the truth in God's Word and write it down opposite that lie or struggle. Every morning, repeat those truths from God's Word before you begin your day. The result? You will cancel the lies and take those thoughts captive, friend!

Wouldn't it be great to live every day in perfect peace? The Bible says it's possible when you trust in God and fix your thoughts on Him. Don't just check off the morning devotions box. While it's great practice, it's not enough. God is with you throughout the day. And while you can't spend all day on your knees in conversation with Him, you *can* keep Him present in your thoughts.

LORD, HELP ME TO ALIGN MY THOUGHTS WITH YOURS.

PRAISE JESUS INSTEAD

The leading priests and the teachers of religious law saw these wonderful miracles and heard even the children in the Temple shouting, "Praise God for the Son of David." But the leaders were indignant. They asked Jesus, "Do you hear what these children are saying?" "Yes," Jesus replied. "Haven't you ever read the Scriptures? For they say, 'You have taught children and infants to give you praise.'"

MATTHEW 21:15–16 NLT

Jesus quoted an Old Testament psalm to the Pharisees that says, "You have taught children and infants to tell of your strength, silencing your enemies and all who oppose you" (Psalm 8:2 NLT).

God loves to hear His children praise Him. Praise can be a powerful weapon. The Bible says it can even silence our enemies.

The next time you are tempted to complain about your struggles, try praising Jesus instead. Processing your feelings with a trusted friend who points you to Jesus is one thing; grumbling about how bad you feel to anyone who listens is another.

Get in the habit of thanking God for what He's done for you instead of complaining. Praise the heavenly Father. Sing to Him! You'll be amazed at how praising God silences the negative thoughts in your head.

LORD, I REPENT OF COMPLAINING ABOUT MY STRUGGLES. HELP ME LEARN TO PRAISE YOU EVEN WHEN I DON'T FEEL LIKE IT.

STRENGTH DURING TEMPTATION

No temptation has overtaken you except what is common to mankind. And God is faithful; he will not let you be tempted beyond what you can bear. But when you are tempted, he will also provide a way out so that you can endure it.

1 CORINTHIANS 10:13 NIV

Think about the things that tempt you most often. Caffeinated drinks? Chocolate? Shopping? Scrolling on social media?

It's easy to dismiss our temptations as "no big deal" when we compare ourselves to others, isn't it? We rationalize that our temptations aren't nearly *that bad* when we know others who struggle with pornography or things we think are "bigger" sins, and so we continue to give in. But overeating and spending too much can easily lead to health and financial problems. Surrendering to temptations of any kind is a big deal.

So, what can you do about it? The Amplified Bible says that God will "provide the way out as well, so that you will be able to endure it [without yielding, and will overcome temptation with joy]."

When you're struggling with temptation, look for the way out—Jesus promises there will always be one. In His strength, you can overcome with joy!

LORD, I REPENT OF COMPARING MY TEMPTATIONS TO OTHERS AND RATIONALIZING MY BEHAVIOR. HELP ME TO LOOK FOR THE WAY OUT SO THAT I CAN JOYFULLY OVERCOME IN YOUR STRENGTH!

MY STRENGTH AND SONG

"See, God has come to save me. I will trust in him and not be afraid. The LORD GOD is my strength and my song; he has given me victory."

ISAIAH 12:2 NLT

It's a leap of faith to sing and praise God during life's hardships. Psalm 32:7 (NIV) says, "You are my hiding place; you will protect me from trouble and surround me with songs of deliverance."

Music is a wonderful gift from God that He created for His people. As we worship Him in praise, it lifts us above our circumstances and transports us to heaven's throne. Hebrews 4:16 (AMP) says, "Therefore let us [with privilege] approach the throne of grace [that is, the throne of God's gracious favor] with confidence and without fear, so that we may receive mercy [for our failures] and find [His amazing] grace to help in time of need [an appropriate blessing, coming just at the right moment]."

The next time you feel like running away from your problems, hide out in Jesus instead. Crank up the praise music and thank Him for His songs of deliverance. Watch and see how He makes a way for you!

LORD, I'M THANKFUL FOR YOUR AMAZING GRACE. I TRUST THAT YOU WILL RESCUE ME FROM MY STRUGGLES AT JUST THE RIGHT MOMENT!

GETTING SOME PERSPECTIVE

"It is He who spreads out the north over emptiness and hangs the earth on nothing. He wraps the waters in His clouds [which otherwise would spill on earth all at once], and the cloud does not burst under them. . . . Yet these are just the fringes of His ways [mere samples of His power], the faintest whisper of His voice! Who can contemplate the thunder of His [full] mighty power?"

JOB 26:7–8, 14 AMP

As you reflect on the great power of God amid hard times, you gain perspective. Imagine Him creating the world and hanging the earth on nothing! And God's Word tells us that this is just a mere sample of His mighty power, only the faintest whisper of His voice.

How amazing that this all-powerful Creator God has His thoughts set on you (Psalm 139). He loves you more than you could ever understand (John 3:16). Ask Him to help you hear His voice. He wants to speak to you. Be listening for Him in all of creation. Notice how this changes your perspective about your life and your circumstances.

LORD, WHEN I LOOK AT ALL YOU'VE DONE, LET IT CHANGE MY HEART. GIVE ME A NEW PERSPECTIVE ON MY CIRCUMSTANCES. I TRUST THAT YOU KNOW WHAT YOU'RE DOING AND THAT YOU'LL TAKE GOOD CARE OF ME.

THE DIRECTOR OF YOUR LIFE

Love God, all you saints; God takes care of all who stay close to him, but he pays back in full those arrogant enough to go it alone. Be brave. Be strong. Don't give up. Expect God to get here soon.

PSALM 31:23–24 MSG

How do you become strong and courageous when what you really feel is weak and afraid instead? You put your hope in the power and strength of the Lord! He takes care of those who stay close to Him.

When you call on Jesus as Lord of your life, you are declaring that He is your director, the one in charge of everything. You are surrendering your will for His. And when you listen for His voice and walk in His ways, He will lead you in all the places you should go.

If you are arrogant and try to control everything on your own, you'll run out of strength. But as God's beloved child, you have His promise that He will thoroughly equip and empower you for everything He wants you to do (2 Timothy 3:17). So that means (1) you never have to worry, and (2) He'll give you the strength you need to get the job done.

I INVITE YOU TO BE THE DIRECTOR OF MY LIFE, LORD. I SURRENDER MY WILL TO YOURS.

SORTING IT OUT WITH JESUS

On the day I called, You answered me; and You made me bold and confident with [renewed] strength in my life.

PSALM 138:3 AMP

How many times have you started and ended a day in utter exhaustion? Does this happen a lot? The Lord wants to renew your strength as you come to Him in prayer.

The Message says this: "Thank you for your love, thank you for your faithfulness; most holy is your name, most holy is your Word. The moment I called out, you stepped in; you made my life large with strength" (Psalm 138:2–3).

Begin by thanking the heavenly Father for His love and faithfulness. Thank Him for His blessings. Thank Him for everything that comes to mind. Thankfulness helps open up your heart to receive. After thanking Him for His goodness, then bring every issue and worry to Him and ask Him to help you sort it out.

Consider writing down all your thoughts and feelings. Once you share them with God, then wait in expectation for Him to answer. Write down what you hear or sense Him saying to you. As you are comforted by your beloved Father, He will fill you with renewed strength and energy to do whatever He has called you to do.

HEAVENLY FATHER, I BRING YOU ALL THE CARES ON MY HEART. WOULD YOU PLEASE HELP ME SORT THEM OUT? PLEASE RENEW MY STRENGTH IN THE PROCESS.

WORSHIP AND STRENGTH

God is awesome in his sanctuary. The God of Israel gives power and strength to his people. Praise be to God!

PSALM 68:35 NLT

The Bible tells us that our awesome God gives us power and strength. He is the God of all creation. And He is *for* you. You are the apple of His eye.

Has it been a while since you've worshipped Him? Why not start making praise your daily practice? Get a list of praise music from church. Download your favorite worship songs. Open your hymnal. Get into the Psalms. However you worship God the best, do it. Whatever sets your mind on things above, make it a daily habit.

Worship the Creator for who He is. Thank Him for all His blessings. Praise Him for being so very good to you. It's amazing how a time of worship can turn your attitude around.

When you worship God, even in the midst of your struggles, something powerful happens! As you turn your gaze away from yourself and toward Jesus, He will strengthen you.

LORD GOD, I WORSHIP YOU, AND I LOVE YOU. I PRAISE YOUR NAME FOR WHO YOU ARE AND FOR ALL YOU'VE DONE. I'M SO THANKFUL FOR YOUR LOVE!

INNER STRENGTH FROM CHRIST

My response is to get down on my knees before the Father, this magnificent Father who parcels out all heaven and earth. I ask him to strengthen you by his Spirit—not a brute strength but a glorious inner strength—that Christ will live in you as you open the door and invite him in.

EPHESIANS 3:14–17 MSG

Look at verse 16 in a few other versions of the Bible:

The Amplified Bible says, "May He grant you out of the riches of His glory, to be strengthened and spiritually energized with power through His Spirit in your inner self, [indwelling your innermost being and personality]."

The New International Version says, "I pray that out of his glorious riches he may strengthen you with power through his Spirit in your inner being,"

Reading the scripture selections in other Bible versions can often help you gain a better understanding of God's Word. If you use a tool like the Blue Letter Bible (found free online), you can also look up the original Hebrew and Greek words to discover their meaning.

From these scriptures in Ephesians 3, we can gather that when God strengthens us, His Spirit indwells us! He gives us a "glorious inner strength" that empowers us through Christ's Spirit Himself.

THANK YOU, HOLY SPIRIT, FOR COMING ALIVE IN ME AND BEING MY TEACHER AND GUIDE! THANK YOU FOR GIVING ME YOUR STRENGTH.

WHY ME?

Moses answered God, "But why me? What makes you think that I could ever go to Pharaoh and lead the children of Israel out of Egypt?" "I'll be with you," God said.

EXODUS 3:11–12 MSG

Moses was a prophet who was chosen by God for great things. Born a Hebrew but raised a prince, Moses eventually ran away from the palace after killing an abusive Egyptian. He hid out in the desert for forty years. Then God spoke to Moses out of the burning bush, asking him to lead His people out of Egypt.

Being called by God was baffling to Moses. He was a Hebrew fugitive, after all. He had killed a man! (Some scholars suggest that Moses may have even had a speech impediment.) Moses couldn't understand why God would ask *him* to go and speak to the most powerful man around and be a leader to all of Israel. Wasn't there someone else more qualified for the job?

Sometimes God asks His people to do hard things—*impossible* things! But He promises to be with us *in* those hard things, proving that our power comes from God and not ourselves (2 Corinthians 4:7).

Have you been asking God, "Why me?" Is He calling you to do something outside of your strength and comfort zone? Be encouraged by Moses' story. God promises to be with you too!

LORD, YOU KNOW THAT I NEED YOU IF I'M EVER GOING TO ACCOMPLISH WHAT YOU'RE CALLING ME TO DO.

FIGHTING BATTLES

"Be strong and courageous! Don't be afraid or discouraged because of the king of Assyria or his mighty army, for there is a power far greater on our side! He may have a great army, but they are merely men. We have the Lord *our God to help us and to fight our battles for us!" Hezekiah's words greatly encouraged the people.*

2 Chronicles 32:7–8 NLT

Hezekiah was facing war. The people of his land needed strength and courage for battle. Hezekiah reminded them of who their God was. And when things looked dire, they cried out to God in prayer. And do you know what God did? He sent an angel who completely wiped out the opposing army. Just like that, it was done!

We can find so much encouragement from the true stories in the Old Testament. God is good—He always has been and always will be. He is all-powerful and creative. And He loves you! Are you bringing your battles to Jesus? Let Him fight for you.

Second Chronicles 32:22 (NIV) says, "So the Lord saved Hezekiah and the people of Jerusalem. . . . He took care of them on every side." Other versions of the Bible say that God gave them rest and peace on every side.

LORD, HELP ME FIGHT MY BATTLES. I'M ASKING YOU TO TAKE CARE OF ME ON EVERY SIDE TOO.

KEEPING MY EYES ON JESUS

But Jesus spoke to them at once. "Don't be afraid," he said. "Take courage. I am here!" Then Peter called to him, "Lord, if it's really you, tell me to come to you, walking on the water." "Yes, come," Jesus said. So Peter went over the side of the boat and walked on the water toward Jesus.

MATTHEW 14:27–29 NLT

You've heard the story. Jesus walks on the water at night. The disciples are in a boat. They see Him and are terrified, thinking they are seeing a ghost. Peter asks Jesus that if it is really Him to call him to come out onto the water. Peter starts walking on the water too! . . . Until he takes his eyes off Jesus.

Have you ever heard Jesus say, "Come," in a situation and then you take a step of faith, but you begin to look around and wonder what on earth you've done? It happens a lot. Reality sets in, and you start to sink.

The great thing about this story is that Jesus was right there. He saw Peter's faith, and then He saw it falter. Peter was terrified when he took his eyes off Jesus. The Bible says that "Jesus immediately reached out and grabbed him" (verse 31 NLT). Trust that He'll reach out for you too.

LORD, HELP ME KEEP MY EYES ON YOU WHEN YOU SAY, "COME."

THE LORD IS CLOSE

"But take courage! None of you will lose your lives, even though the ship will go down. For last night an angel of the God to whom I belong and whom I serve stood beside me, and he said, 'Don't be afraid, Paul. . . . God in his goodness has granted safety to everyone sailing with you.'"

ACTS 27:22–24 NLT

In the book of Acts, Paul was arrested and put in prison several times even though he was innocent. In Acts 27 we hear about his shipwreck. He was headed to Rome for his trial. God sent an angel to encourage Paul in this desperate time.

Life can be so hard sometimes. We lose a loved one or a relationship or a ministry. Sometimes the ship goes down. But God is *always* faithful to His people.

Psalm 34:18 (NIV) says, "The LORD is close to the brokenhearted and saves those who are crushed in spirit." He is with you in the storm, and He is with you when the ship goes down. Even if you were part of the cause.

If you're in the middle of some desperate times, be encouraged. God is close.

LORD, I NEED TO KNOW THAT YOU'RE CLOSE. MY HEART IS HEAVY AND BURDENED. PLEASE SHOW ME THAT YOU'RE NEAR AND THAT YOU SEE ME.

EVERYTHING YOU'LL EVER NEED

For to us a Child is born, to us a Son is given; and the government shall be upon His shoulder, and His name shall be called Wonderful Counselor, Mighty God, Everlasting Father [of Eternity], Prince of Peace.

ISAIAH 9:6 AMPC

Sixteenth-century Bible scholar William Tyndale said of Jesus, "He is our Redeemer, Deliverer, Reconciler, Mediator, Intercessor, Advocate, Attorney, Solicitor, our Hope, Comfort, Shield, Protection, Defender, Strength, Health, Satisfaction and Salvation. His blood, his death, all that he ever did, is ours. And Christ himself, with all that he is or can do, is ours. . . . And God (as great as he is) is mine, with all that he hath, through Christ and his purchasing."

What a list! Everything you'll ever need is yours in Christ Jesus. You don't have to work for it. You can do nothing to earn it. The only thing you need to do is receive it. You need an advocate? You have one. You need strength and health and satisfaction? Let Jesus fill you with those things.

Psalm 37:4 (AMP) says, "Delight yourself in the LORD, and He will give you the desires and petitions of your heart." As you spend time in God's presence, your every need will be taken care of.

JESUS, SHOW ME WHAT IT MEANS TO DELIGHT MYSELF IN YOU. THANK YOU FOR TAKING CARE OF MY EVERY NEED.

OUR DEFENDER AND PROTECTOR

I look up to the mountains; does my strength come from mountains? No, my strength comes from God, who made heaven, and earth, and mountains. . . . God guards you from every evil, he guards your very life. He guards you when you leave and when you return, he guards you now, he guards you always.

Psalm 121:1–2, 7–8 MSG

It's easy to get defensive when you are criticized. Ever struggle with that? Defensiveness is like a shield of self-protection. In the movie *War Room*, Miss Clara declares that God is a good defense attorney if you'll let Him be one. You can trust Him to defend and protect you.

The Bible tells us that the heavenly Father guards us and that our strength comes from the maker of heaven and earth. Remember, you won't find strength by digging down deep and mustering it yourself. Supernatural strength and courage come from God alone. He is the very source of life and power.

Does this mean you can stop trying to manipulate circumstances and people to protect yourself? Yes! God is your guardian and protector. He will give you the courage and strength to do whatever it is He asks of you. And sometimes it's simply to rest in Him.

YOU ARE MY DEFENDER, LORD.
THANK YOU FOR GUARDING AND PROTECTING ME.

BLAMELESS

May God himself, the God of peace, sanctify you through and through. May your whole spirit, soul and body be kept blameless at the coming of our Lord Jesus Christ. The one who calls you is faithful, and he will do it.

1 THESSALONIANS 5:23–24 NIV

Making mistakes is part of life. We teach this to children, but why are we so hard on ourselves when we mess up? When you start criticizing or attacking yourself for making a mistake, remember the truth of who God says you are.

If you are struggling with being overly critical of yourself, try this: Think of someone you dearly love. Maybe a daughter or sister or best friend. If they were in the same situation that you are in, what advice would you give them? Would you beat them up with your words? Would you criticize everything they've done? Surely not! Now be kind to yourself just like that.

Because of Jesus' death and resurrection, God sees you as blameless and pure. Jesus took on all of your sin and shame, and He paid for it dearly, once and for all. So, you can face any accusation, whether it's from yourself or others, with truth from God's Word.

LORD, HELP ME TO DEFEAT ANY LIES ABOUT MYSELF WITH TRUTH FROM YOUR WORD.

THE LIFTER OF YOUR HEAD

Set your minds on things above, not on earthly things. For you died, and your life is now hidden with Christ in God. When Christ, who is your life, appears, then you also will appear with him in glory.

COLOSSIANS 3:2–4 NIV

Struggling with insecurity? It's normal to feel "less than" in our worldly culture! But remember this: Your security comes from Christ alone. Yes, you have the promise of heaven someday. But Jesus came so that you could also know security here and now.

When you set your mind on things above, God gives you an eternal perspective of your life. You see people as eternal and things as temporary. The eternal becomes so much more important than the material.

If you struggle with shame because you can't afford the latest fashions or you live in a humble home instead of an impressive estate, take heart. Things really don't matter.

Psalm 3:3 (NIV) says, "But you, LORD, are a shield around me, my glory, the One who lifts my head high." You are covered, secure, made new and alive in Christ, now and forever. No more feeling inferior, friend. Lift your head.

JESUS, I NEED AN ETERNAL PERSPECTIVE.
PLEASE LIFT MY HEAD TO GAZE IN YOUR DIRECTION.

TRUSTING GOD'S WORD

No, in all these things we are more than conquerors through him who loved us. For I am convinced that neither death nor life, neither angels nor demons, neither the present nor the future, nor any powers, neither height nor depth, nor anything else in all creation, will be able to separate us from the love of God that is in Christ Jesus our Lord.

ROMANS 8:37–39 NIV

We are more than conquerors through Christ. Nothing can ever separate us from His love.

Let those words sink in for a moment. The truth of God's Word is staggering to those of us who follow Christ. If Christians lived out the truth of this scripture every day, if they walked in the courage that Christ says is ours, it would change everything.

What would that look like? It would look like families loving Jesus together and serving Him. It would look like fears defeated and Christians boldly living out the calling that God gave them. It would look like churches being grounded in truth and loving one another well, drawing the outsiders in!

God's Word can change everything. It *will* change everything—if you believe it.

JESUS, I WANT TO WALK IN YOUR TRUTH.
HELP ME TO LIVE THIS OUT EVERY DAY.
FORGIVE ME FOR MY UNBELIEF AT TIMES.
GIVE ME THE COURAGE TO TRUST YOUR WORD.

ROMANTIC STRUGGLES

For in Christ lives all the fullness of God in a human body. So you also are complete through your union with Christ, who is the head over every ruler and authority.

COLOSSIANS 2:9–10 NLT

"You complete me." Weddings. Love songs. Romance movies. Our culture has often taught us that there is one person out there who will complete us.

But God never meant for any of us to put that responsibility on another human being. It's too much for human shoulders. People will often fail us and let us down. And then what? When we depend on another human to be our everything, we will be sorely disappointed.

If you are struggling in a romantic relationship because you've been disappointed by the one you thought was supposed to complete you, know this: You are complete in Christ alone. Only Jesus has shoulders big enough to carry you. Only Jesus can meet all your needs and fill you with lasting joy and peace.

When you are whole in Christ, you can be in relationship with others in healthy and loving ways, with mutual responsibility for the success of the relationship, each of you moving toward Christ. When that happens, you move toward each other too.

LORD, FORGIVE ME FOR WHEN I'VE PUT TOO MUCH RESPONSIBILITY ON THE SHOULDERS OF OTHERS TO COMPLETE ME. I AM WHOLE IN YOU ALONE.

TRUST IN EACH MOMENT

"For the Holy Spirit will teach you at that time what you should say."

LUKE 12:12 NIV

Have you ever been asked to pray in public? What about giving a speech? Or maybe there's an upcoming conversation that you are dreading. Whatever it is, Jesus wants to help.

In Luke 12, Jesus tells His disciples not to worry about what to say or how they will defend themselves when they are brought before public officials and church leaders. He didn't want them bogged down with the kind of worry that takes energy away from more important tasks. He wanted them to know they could trust Him in the moment to tell them what to say.

You can trust Jesus in each moment too. The next time you find yourself in an intimidating situation, trust Jesus. If Christ is alive in you, then He is at work. If He wants you to do or say something in a certain situation, you can trust Him to let you know. And you don't have to worry about it ahead of time. This will take some practice. Whenever you're headed into a stressful situation, be present with God the entire time. Invite Him to speak to you. Tell Him how you're feeling. Then leave it in His very capable hands.

LORD, HELP ME TRUST YOU IN EACH MOMENT.

SO WORRIED

Don't worry about anything; instead, pray about everything. Tell God what you need, and thank him for all he has done. Then you will experience God's peace, which exceeds anything we can understand. His peace will guard your hearts and minds as you live in Christ Jesus.

PHILIPPIANS 4:6–7 NLT

"I'm so worried about (fill in the blank)." How many times this week have you caught yourself or someone else saying those words? Worry. It's an epidemic.

Why did Jesus tell us not to worry (check out Matthew 6:25–34)? When you hold worries inside of you, they can actually cause harm to your body. Jesus asks, "Can any one of you by worrying add a single hour to your life?" (Matthew 6:27 NIV). The answer is no. And the opposite is often true! Worry causes stress—and stress is a killer.

God wants you to bring your fears and worries to Him instead. He promises that when you do, a very powerful thing happens: He'll give you His peace in place of your worry.

God's peace is so powerful that it doesn't make sense to anyone else but you and Him. The heavenly Father wants you to be thankful instead of stressed, and He alone can help you with that.

GOD, I REPENT OF THE SIN OF WORRYING! TEACH ME TO PRAY AND TRUST YOU INSTEAD.

STRUGGLING WITH SIN

But there is another power within me that is at war with my mind. This power makes me a slave to the sin that is still within me. Oh, what a miserable person I am! Who will free me from this life that is dominated by sin and death? Thank God! The answer is in Jesus Christ our Lord.

ROMANS 7:23–25 NLT

Take a few minutes to read what the apostle Paul wrote in Romans 7:15–25 (NIV).

"I do not understand what I do. . ." Can you relate? Ever find yourself gossiping again after you confessed only yesterday? Criticizing your husband or children instead of building them up? Or maybe an addiction has taken hold and you can't seem to shake free from it.

You find yourself slipping into old sin patterns, thinking negatively about yourself or others, feeling down. What then? Romans 7 echoes this very humanness.

The answer is at the start of the very next chapter: "So now there is no condemnation for those who belong to Christ Jesus. And because you belong to him, the power of the life-giving Spirit has freed you from the power of sin that leads to death" (Romans 8:1–2 NLT). You can start again.

JESUS, THANK YOU FOR THE TRUTH THAT I AM NOT CONDEMNED. PLEASE GIVE ME THE POWER TO START OVER. SEND ME THE ACCOUNTABILITY I NEED TO SUCCEED.

INTIMIDATION

Therefore if you have been raised with Christ [to a new life, sharing in His resurrection from the dead], keep seeking the things that are above, where Christ is, seated at the right hand of God. Set your mind and keep focused habitually on the things above [the heavenly things], not on things that are on the earth [which have only temporal value].

Colossians 3:1–2 AMP

When are you most intimidated? Take a minute and think about that. Is it when you must do a certain job or task? Being around a particular person? Perhaps it's when the in-laws come for a visit. (Did you finish cleaning the underside of all the toilets? Is the inside of the microwave splattered?)

Intimidating situations and people come at us often. You will get lots of practice with this one!

In the moment when anxious feelings come, ask Jesus to give you a calm and a peace that comes from focusing on Him. As the situation unfolds or the intimidating person speaks, invite Jesus to give you an eternal perspective of the person or situation. Be on the lookout for what He wants to show you.

JESUS, HELP ME TO KEEP MY EYES ON YOU AND LISTEN AS YOU SHOW ME YOUR PERSPECTIVE. HELP ME TO LOVE THE PEOPLE IN FRONT OF ME, EVEN WHEN THEY ARE INTIMIDATING.

JOY AND PEACE IN HIS PRESENCE

A happy heart is good medicine and a joyful mind causes healing, but a broken spirit dries up the bones.

PROVERBS 17:22 AMP

Stress is hard on a body, both physically and mentally. Extended and unrelenting stress can cause heart problems and even death. God does not want us to carry all of that on our shoulders. It's too much. It leads to the broken spirit that "dries up the bones."

But the truth is that life is hard and traumatic things will happen. Does God want you to just sweep it all under the rug and put on a happy face? Surely not. Jesus invites you to come to Him with everything. As you give Him permission to heal your hurts and heartaches, He supernaturally gives you rest and peace—the kind of peace that "transcends all understanding" (Philippians 4:7 NIV).

As you spend more and more time in God's presence, He shows you the right path and fills you with joy! Psalm 16:11 (NIV) says, "You make known to me the path of life; you will fill me with joy in your presence, with eternal pleasures at your right hand."

I'M STRESSED, LORD. I'VE ALLOWED THE WEIGHT OF THIS WORLD TO BRING ME DOWN. I NEED MORE OF YOUR PRESENCE IN MY LIFE. PLEASE FILL ME WITH YOUR JOY AND PEACE AS I SPEND TIME WITH YOU.

ENTERTAINMENT STRUGGLES

How can a young person live a clean life? By carefully reading the map of your Word. I'm single-minded in pursuit of you; don't let me miss the road signs you've posted. I've banked your promises in the vault of my heart so I won't sin myself bankrupt.

PSALM 119:9–11 MSG

Do you ever struggle with entertainment choices? Our culture is hypersexualized and full of darkness. It can be so hard to remain pure in thought and action with impurity constantly staring us right in the face. Even when we're not looking for it, it comes and seeks us out!

Psalm 101:3 (AMP) makes it clear what we, as believers, need to do: "I will set no worthless or wicked thing before my eyes. I hate the practice of those who fall away [from the right path]; it will not grasp hold of me."

The Bible gives us hope that no matter our age, we can still live a pure life amid the battle. When we store up the promises of God by reading and knowing the truth of His Word, God gives us the power to avoid sin. Psalm 119:11 (NIV) says, "I have hidden your word in my heart that I might not sin against you."

LORD, I REPENT OF WATCHING INAPPROPRIATE ENTERTAINMENT. HELP ME HIDE YOUR WORD IN MY HEART AND LIVE A LIFE OF PURITY.

A NEW THING

"Do not remember the former things, or ponder the things of the past. Listen carefully, I am about to do a new thing, now it will spring forth; will you not be aware of it? I will even put a road in the wilderness, rivers in the desert."

ISAIAH 43:18–19 AMP

We all have things in our past that we'd like to forget. An awkward and embarrassing moment. A heated conversation. A public failure. These memories often replay themselves in our minds. Jesus doesn't want you to keep carrying those burdens around, friend. You can't fix everything, and you can't fix other people—but you *can* fix your mind on Christ: "Forgetting what is behind and straining toward what is ahead, I press on toward the goal to win the prize for which God has called me heavenward in Christ Jesus" (Philippians 3:13–14 NIV).

Let Jesus do something new in your life! Spend some time bringing all your difficult memories to Him. They need resolved in your mind so that you can move on. Ask Jesus to wash them in His mercy and grace. He is with you in each moment and every memory. He can rewrite the script you play in your mind.

JESUS, I'M READY FOR A NEW THING. TAKE MY PAST AND HELP ME REWRITE THE SCRIPT SO I DON'T PLAY THOSE OLD MESSAGES ANYMORE.

STRUGGLING WITH HOLINESS?

So roll up your sleeves, get your head in the game, be totally ready to receive the gift that's coming when Jesus arrives. Don't lazily slip back into those old grooves of evil, doing just what you feel like doing. You didn't know any better then; you do now. As obedient children, let yourselves be pulled into a way of life shaped by God's life, a life energetic and blazing with holiness. God said, "I am holy; you be holy."

1 PETER 1:13–16 MSG

First Peter 1:16 (NIV) says, "Be holy, because I am holy." At first glance, that sounds impossible! How can I possibly be holy? Second Corinthians 5:21 (NIV) says, "God made him who had no sin to be sin for us, so that in him we might become the righteousness of God."

The Christian life is not a set of rules you must follow to please God. That's religion. The difference in following Jesus is that His Spirit is alive in you. That's where the power comes from to live the Christian life! Jesus Himself is your righteousness, your holiness! You don't have to muster strength on your own. Holiness is only possible through His Spirit alive and at work in you.

JESUS, SHAPE MY LIFE TO BE LIKE YOURS. THANK YOU FOR ALL THAT YOU'VE DONE TO MAKE ME RIGHT WITH GOD! I LOVE YOU, JESUS!

CONTROL ISSUES

"The Lord *himself goes before you and will be with you; he will never leave you nor forsake you. Do not be afraid; do not be discouraged."*

Deuteronomy 31:8 NIV

The Message words Deuteronomy 31:7–8 this way: "Be strong. Take courage. . . . God is striding ahead of you. He's right there with you. He won't let you down; he won't leave you. Don't be intimidated. Don't worry."

Are you struggling with any fears today? Sometimes fear can come from feeling like things are beyond your control. Firstborn children tend to struggle with control. People who have unresolved trauma often struggle with control. And people who have been hurt deeply by a spouse, close friend, or family member often have this struggle too.

The truth is you are not in control of the world or the people you love. And that's okay. It's actually good! When you surrender your control issues to Jesus, it may feel scary. But when you've done it—truly surrendered your control issues—you will feel a huge sense of relief!

God is going ahead of you. He has the whole world in His hands. He won't leave you! He may not direct the world like you would like Him to sometimes, but He is good. And you can trust Him fully!

I SURRENDER MY CONTROL ISSUES TO YOU, JESUS. HELP ME TRUST YOU COMPLETELY!

THE BLEEDING WOMAN

Just then a woman who had been subject to bleeding for twelve years came up behind him and touched the edge of his cloak. She said to herself, "If I only touch his cloak, I will be healed."

MATTHEW 9:20–21 NIV

In Bible times, menstruating women were considered "unclean" and had many restrictions about what they could do, who they could touch, and more. An unclean person couldn't go to the temple. Being "unclean" wasn't a sin, but it did come with a burden and regulations about how to become clean again. The bleeding had to stop first, and then they had to wash.

Imagine bleeding for twelve years and being considered unclean for that entire time—that's an entire 4,380 days! You couldn't go to church. A man couldn't touch you. You were constantly washing. No doubt this woman was desperate, exhausted, and lonely.

Verse 22 (NIV) says, "Jesus turned and saw her. 'Take heart, daughter,' he said, 'your faith has healed you.' And the woman was healed at that moment."

Mark 5 tells the same story: "He said to her, 'Daughter, your faith has healed you. Go in peace and be freed from your suffering'" (verse 34 NIV).

When we need healing, we can have faith in the mighty power of Jesus.

LORD, I NEED A TOUCH FROM YOU.
I TRUST YOU TO HEAL ME.

BEYOND YOUR WILDEST DREAMS

Now to him who is able to do immeasurably more than all we ask or imagine, according to his power that is at work within us, to him be glory in the church and in Christ Jesus throughout all generations, for ever and ever! Amen.

EPHESIANS 3:20–21 NIV

When God's power is at work within you, the possibilities are beyond your imagination. *The Message* puts it this way: "God can do anything, you know—far more than you could ever imagine or guess or request in your wildest dreams!"

Whatever struggle you are facing right now—big or small—God cares. As you pray about it, don't put God in a box, thinking that there's no way out or that there's only one right answer that you'll never figure out.

Trust this: God is *always* going before you. Psalm 139:5 (NIV) says, "You hem me in behind and before, and you lay your hand upon me."

God's ways are not our ways (Isaiah 55:8), and His response just might be beyond your understanding. Things aren't always what they seem, and God can change your problems and struggles into something beautiful if you let Him.

LORD, I WANT TO BELIEVE THAT MY STRUGGLES WILL TURN OUT OKAY. HELP ME TO TRUST YOU.

YOU'RE THERE

Is there anyplace I can go to avoid your Spirit? to be out of your sight? If I climb to the sky, you're there! If I go underground, you're there! If I flew on morning's wings to the far western horizon, you'd find me in a minute—you're already there waiting! Then I said to myself, "Oh, he even sees me in the dark! At night I'm immersed in the light!" It's a fact: darkness isn't dark to you; night and day, darkness and light, they're all the same to you.

PSALM 139:7–12 MSG

God has promised to be with you in everything. Wherever you go, whatever you do, He's there. He will never leave you (Matthew 28:20; Hebrews 13:5). If He asks you to go somewhere or do something, He'll always provide exactly what you need at the right time. And you can count on Him to keep His promises. He is always going before you and working everything out for your good.

Psalm 139:9–10 (NIV) says, "If I rise on the wings of the dawn, if I settle on the far side of the sea, even there your hand will guide me, your right hand will hold me fast."

God's hand is guiding you and holding you fast. That's a promise you can cling to.

FATHER, I WILL CLING TO YOU AND YOUR PROMISES!

NEW STRENGTH

He gives strength to the weary and increases the power of the weak. Even youths grow tired and weary, and young men stumble and fall; but those who hope in the LORD will renew their strength. They will soar on wings like eagles; they will run and not grow weary, they will walk and not be faint.

ISAIAH 40:29–31 NIV

Could you use an extra-large helping of God's strength and power in your life? The Bible says that those who wait for and hope in the Lord—the people who pray—will gain new strength!

God will provide strength and power to us when we feel like we don't have any—we just need to go to Him in prayer and then wait expectantly. Waiting for the Lord in prayer means that we expect Him to show up and keep His promises. It's not wishful thinking. It's a deep knowing that God is at work in our lives, orchestrating everything for our good and for His glory. Romans 8:28 (NIV) makes us that promise: "We know that in all things God works for the good of those who love him, who have been called according to his purpose."

I COME TO YOU EXPECTANTLY, LORD. PLEASE RENEW MY STRENGTH. I KNOW IT COMES FROM YOU ALONE. I'M SO THANKFUL YOU'RE AT WORK IN MY LIFE.

STAY ALERT

Stay alert! Watch out for your great enemy, the devil. He prowls around like a roaring lion, looking for someone to devour. Stand firm against him, and be strong in your faith. Remember that your family of believers all over the world is going through the same kind of suffering you are.

1 PETER 5:8–9 NLT

The enemy knows he has already been defeated by Jesus. Colossians 2:15 (NLT) says, "In this way, he disarmed the spiritual rulers and authorities. He shamed them publicly by his victory over them on the cross."

Even though Satan knows he has been defeated, he's still trying his best to get into your head and discourage you so you won't be able to live your best for Jesus. That's why God's Word tells us to stay alert.

Don't fall for Satan's tricks. He is the father of lies (John 8:44). You have power in the name of Jesus to get rid of any evil coming after you. James 4:7 (NIV) says, "Submit yourselves, then, to God. Resist the devil, and he will flee from you."

You don't have to be afraid; just stay alert. Don't focus on your fear of the enemy. Instead, focus on Jesus and His power to fight your battles!

LORD, I TRUST THAT I AM NEVER ALONE IN MY STRUGGLES. IN YOUR STRENGTH, I WILL NOT FEAR. HELP ME STAY ALERT.

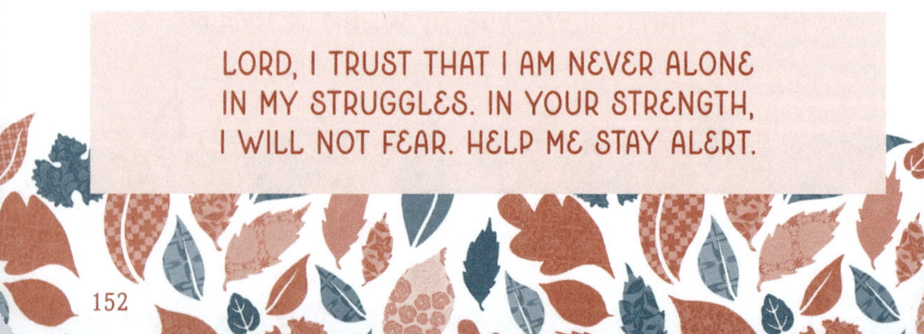

NEVER GIVE UP

Those who live only to satisfy their own sinful nature will harvest decay and death from that sinful nature. But those who live to please the Spirit will harvest everlasting life from the Spirit. So let's not get tired of doing what is good. At just the right time we will reap a harvest of blessing if we don't give up.

GALATIANS 6:8–9 NLT

During the grueling process of Navy SEAL training, candidates can "ring the bell" three times to let others know they are quitting. This happens because they've run out of their own strength. The training is utterly exhausting both physically and emotionally. When these candidates feel they have nothing left to give, they ring the bell. The fact is that most candidates do not make it through SEAL training.

As followers of Jesus, we never need to depend on our own strength to get us through the sometimes-grueling demands of life. We depend on His. And His strength never runs out!

Remember that the heavenly Father's power shines through in our weakness (2 Corinthians 12:9). Allow Him to be your strength. Choose Him! Keep coming back to God every day in prayer, trusting that He will fill you with His strength anew. You will reap a harvest of blessing in the process.

LORD, I'M SO GRATEFUL THAT YOUR STRENGTH IS ALWAYS IN FRESH SUPPLY!

COMPLETELY HONEST

I pray to you, O LORD, my rock. Do not turn a deaf ear to me. For if you are silent, I might as well give up and die. Listen to my prayer for mercy as I cry out to you for help, as I lift my hands toward your holy sanctuary.

PSALM 28:1–2 NLT

You can be completely honest with God. You can't hide anything from Him anyway. For a good taste of this, read the Psalms. They are full of brutal honesty and raw emotion.

God is the safest place for you to share everything. And He is the best place to go when you need help sorting out your raw emotions. He can shine His light on all your thoughts and feelings and help you work them in the very best way.

Check out Psalm 88:6–9 (NLT): "You have thrown me into the lowest pit, into the darkest depths. Your anger weighs me down; with wave after wave you have engulfed me. You have driven my friends away by making me repulsive to them. I am in a trap with no way of escape. My eyes are blinded by my tears." How's that for brutal honesty? The answer is found at the end of verse 9: "Each day I beg for your help, O LORD; I lift my hands to you for mercy."

LORD, HELP ME TO BE COMPLETELY HONEST WITH YOU AS WE WORK THROUGH MY STRUGGLES TOGETHER.

GIVE THANKS IN THE STRUGGLE

Rejoice always and delight in your faith; be unceasing and persistent in prayer; in every situation [no matter what the circumstances] be thankful and continually give thanks to God; for this is the will of God for you in Christ Jesus.

1 THESSALONIANS 5:16–18 AMP

These scriptures about rejoicing and praying can be difficult pills to swallow—especially during times of grief and heartache. One Bible commentary states that Paul was saying not that we should thank God *for* everything but rather that we should thank God *in* everything. See the difference?

People often wonder what God's will is for them. First Thessalonians 5:16–18 lays it all out in black and white! Rejoice always and pray continually. Where do we get the strength and power to do that? From Jesus Christ Himself. From being in His presence. From trusting that He will never leave us no matter what the circumstances are.

This is not fake happiness. It is a smile through the tears. Joy in sorrow. Authenticity during the heartache. The faith that prevails.

Having an attitude of thankfulness in all circumstances shows the world that Jesus is alive and at work in us always. This changes hearts, homes, and entire communities!

JESUS, PLEASE TEACH ME HOW TO REJOICE AND BE THANKFUL NO MATTER MY CIRCUMSTANCES! COME ALIVE IN ME!

STRENGTH, HOPE, AND SAFETY

For God alone my soul waits in silence and quietly submits to Him, for my hope is from Him.

PSALM 62:5 AMP

Psalm 62 is a great reminder that we can find our safety and strength in God alone. Verses 7 and 8 (MSG) say this: "My help and glory are in God—granite-strength and safe-harbor-God—So trust him absolutely, people; lay your lives on the line for him. God is a safe place to be."

Thank the heavenly Father for being a safe place for you. When you mess up and when you succeed, He is your refuge. He delights in you. He shares your sorrows and your joys. Allow Him to be with you in those times. Bring your successes and failures to Jesus and let Him love you in them. You don't have to perform for God. He sees you just as you are, and He loves you anyway.

Verse 11 (MSG) says, "God said this once and for all; how many times have I heard it repeated? 'Strength comes straight from God.'"

God is the very source of strength that you've been needing, friend. He has all the answers you're looking for. He is your safe place. Sit quietly before Him and allow Him to fill you with hope and strength for this day.

THANK YOU FOR BEING MY REFUGE, LORD!

STRUGGLING WITH DOUBT

And [so that you will begin to know] what the immeasurable and unlimited and surpassing greatness of His [active, spiritual] power is in us who believe.

EPHESIANS 1:19 AMP

Struggling with doubt is a big deal. We all go through it from time to time. Is God still there? Is He even real?

Job 36:26 (NLT) says, "Look, God is greater than we can understand." And Isaiah 55:8–9 (NLT) says, "'My thoughts are nothing like your thoughts,' says the LORD. 'And my ways are far beyond anything you could imagine. For just as the heavens are higher than the earth, so my ways are higher than your ways and my thoughts higher than your thoughts.'"

The Bible tells us that the power of God is unlimited! Do you believe that this applies to His power in your own life too? It does! Ask God to write this truth on your heart. It's a prayer He loves to answer. If you are struggling with doubt, bring it to Jesus. Ask Him if there are any lies you might be believing that could be preventing you from accepting the truth of His limitless power in your life.

LORD, YOUR WAYS ARE FAR BEYOND WHAT I CAN UNDERSTAND, BUT I PRAY THAT YOU'LL HELP ME BEGIN TO UNDERSTAND WHO YOU REALLY ARE.

OUR GENTLE SHEPHERD

"If a man has a hundred sheep and one of them wanders away, what will he do? Won't he leave the ninety-nine others on the hills and go out to search for the one that is lost? And if he finds it, I tell you the truth, he will rejoice over it more than over the ninety-nine that didn't wander away! In the same way, it is not my heavenly Father's will that even one of these little ones should perish."

MATTHEW 18:12–14 NLT

Good shepherds don't want to lose any of their sheep. In John 10:11 (NIV), Jesus tells us, "I am the good shepherd. The good shepherd lays down his life for the sheep." Jesus is our good shepherd, and you matter so much to Him that if you ever go wandering off, He'll search for you too!

Are you struggling to stay on the straight and narrow path? Trust that Jesus is coming for you. He wants you close and will lead you to the right place. When you wander off, you could get lost, hurt, or confused. So, allow Jesus to come for you. He is gentle and won't force His way upon you. Will you let Him lead you back to Him?

JESUS, I WANT TO REMAIN CLOSE TO YOU. PLEASE COME FOR ME. LEAD ME ON THE RIGHT PATH.

KNOWING GOD'S VOICE

"My sheep listen to my voice; I know them, and they follow me."

JOHN 10:27 NLT

We've established that Jesus is our good shepherd and we are His sheep. Psalm 95:7 (NLT) says, "For he is our God. We are the people he watches over, the flock under his care. If only you would listen to his voice today!"

Do you know His voice? Do you hear Him speaking to you? God primarily speaks to us through His Word. We can also hear from God in creation (Psalm 19:1–4) or through music or a song in church or on the radio (Ephesians 5:19). We can also hear from God through our pastors and other Christians. When God is speaking, He reminds us of His Word (John 14:26). He will never say anything contrary to His truth.

Start listening for His voice in your life. Ask Him to remind you of His Word and to confirm that what you're hearing is from God. Sometimes you'll hear the same thing again and again when God wants you to know something specific at the right time. You'll read a scripture. Then you'll hear it somewhere else—maybe in a song. Then you'll hear it again from another source. Pay attention when that happens! You might be hearing God's voice!

LORD, HELP ME TO RECOGNIZE YOUR VOICE IN MY LIFE!

PLANNING FOR THE FUTURE

In all your ways know and acknowledge and recognize Him, and He will make your paths straight and smooth [removing obstacles that block your way].

PROVERBS 3:6 AMP

This proverb is a great reminder that God can take a path that looks rocky and daunting and make it smooth by the time you get to it! Worrying about the future is pointless because God can change all the circumstances before it actually happens. That's why the Bible warns us against worry—it can steal moments of our lives that we can't get back.

When you acknowledge God as you plan for the future, He can remove obstacles. Decision-making is not always as difficult as we make it. When we forget that God wants to help us make life choices, we become confused and anxious. When we leave God out of the decision-making process, it causes lots of unnecessary problems and worries. Have you left God out? Confess that to Him in prayer. Ask His forgiveness. Ask Him to help transform your thinking in this area. Then listen for His voice as you go about your day. He'll be with you, leading you in the right direction.

LORD, I REPENT OF PICTURING THE FUTURE WITHOUT ACKNOWLEDGING THAT YOU'RE IN CONTROL! I CHOOSE NOT TO WORRY. I TRUST THAT YOU HAVE GREAT PLANS FOR ME.

LIFE ON THE ROCK

"Therefore everyone who hears these words of mine and puts them into practice is like a wise man who built his house on the rock. The rain came down, the streams rose, and the winds blew and beat against that house; yet it did not fall, because it had its foundation on the rock."

MATTHEW 7:24–25 NIV

Beach houses are lovely and great places to spend a vacation. But it's always risky to build a house on the sand against the backdrop of the vast and powerful ocean. If that water gets super angry, the beach house may not stand a chance. Vacation rental? Yes, please! Building your family's only home in the sand by the sea? Maybe pray about that first!

Jesus tells this story in Matthew to teach us about life as a follower of Christ. If we build our lives on the firm foundation of Jesus, we won't fall apart when hard things happen. We trust in God and have experienced His love at work in us! But if we don't have a solid foundation on Jesus—not knowing or believing and obeying His truth for our lives—we can fall apart when storms and bad things happen to us, like a vacation home toppling over in the sand.

LORD, I PUT MY TRUST IN YOU—MY SOLID ROCK.

UNLIMITED POWER AND LOVE

But the L*ORD* *is the only true God. He is the living God and the everlasting King! . . . But the* L*ORD* *made the earth by his power, and he preserves it by his wisdom. With his own understanding he stretched out the heavens. When he speaks in the thunder, the heavens roar with rain. He causes the clouds to rise over the earth. He sends the lightning with the rain and releases the wind from his storehouses.*

JEREMIAH 10:10, 12–13 NLT

The God who loves and cares about you is the same God who stretched out the heavens. Imagine that as you pray! Can you envision His greatness and majesty? Can you picture Him sending the lightning with His mighty hands and opening the storehouses to release the winds?

It might be hard to believe that you matter so much to God, but the Bible tells us it's true. When you think about God's unlimited power and His love for you, do you trust that God can handle anything you have going on? He knows your struggles. He sees your pain.

HEAVENLY FATHER, IF YOU CAN SPEAK WATER INTO EXISTENCE AT THE SOUND OF YOUR VOICE, I KNOW YOU CAN TAKE CARE OF EVERYTHING I'M STRUGGLING WITH. I TRUST YOU TO HELP ME, LORD.

THE DOOR IS OPEN

"So I say to you: Ask and it will be given to you; seek and you will find; knock and the door will be opened to you. For everyone who asks receives; the one who seeks finds; and to the one who knocks, the door will be opened."

LUKE 11:9–10 NIV

It just makes sense to call a wise friend when you need advice. And that can be a great thing to do when the time is right. But many times we forget to bring things to God first. We try to get our needs met through other people and other sources when God is waiting for us to come to Him.

James 4:2 (NIV) says, "You do not have because you do not ask God." Wow! If we would only learn to go to God with our needs and requests, we would be amazed at how much He wants to show up in our lives. We can ask for anything. And, as we come to Him in prayer, He aligns our hearts to His. He shows up in ways we could never imagine (Ephesians 3:20). He opens the door.

LORD JESUS, I REPENT OF GOING TO OTHERS BEFORE I COME TO YOU. PLEASE TRAIN MY HEART AND MIND TO SEEK YOU FIRST.

GOD CARES ABOUT YOUR TEARS

You have taken account of my wanderings; put my tears in Your bottle. Are they not recorded in Your book? Then my enemies will turn back in the day when I call; this I know, that God is for me.

Psalm 56:8–9 AMP

God cares about the things you care about. Psalm 139 is a reminder of how intimately He knows you. The Bible says He even counts your tears and keeps track of them.

Isaiah 53:3 (NLT) says, "He was despised and rejected—a man of sorrows, acquainted with deepest grief. We turned our backs on him and looked the other way. He was despised, and we did not care."

Jesus was called the "Man of Sorrows" because He was rejected by people (many who rejected Him were His own family and closest friends) and was very familiar with pain and sadness. Whatever you're going through, Jesus understands because He's been there. Have you ever felt left out or not good enough for other people? Are you going through a particularly difficult heartache? Talk to God about it. Your tears matter to Him. The Bible says He is *for* you. He's on your side. You are never alone.

MY HEART IS HURTING, LORD. THANK YOU FOR UNDERSTANDING MY HEARTACHE. I'M SO THANKFUL THAT YOU CARE.

EVEN AT NIGHT

I will bless the Lord *who guides me; even at night my heart instructs me. I know the* Lord *is always with me. I will not be shaken, for he is right beside me. No wonder my heart is glad, and I rejoice. My body rests in safety.*

Psalm 16:7–9 NLT

A woman who'd been going through a very difficult time kept waking up in the middle of the night. As she woke, she heard a song in her heart and mind that reminded her that she wasn't alone. She realized that God was singing over her as scripture says in Zephaniah 3:17!

This woman developed an eternal perspective and began to see problems and heartache in their proper light. She knew that weeping may last for a little while, but joy would come (Psalm 30:5). Her struggles didn't disappear, but she realized that she wasn't alone in them. Jesus was with her in supernatural ways, and He kept singing over her in the night through her trials.

You don't have to be shaken when trials come. Jesus is with you always. Bring any sadness or heartache to Him. He wants to help carry your load. He wants to sing over you too.

LORD, I WANT TO KNOW YOU'RE HERE AND THAT YOU SEE ME. PLEASE GUIDE ME AND SHOW ME THAT YOU'RE NEAR.

A DEEP SOUL REST

"Come to me, all you who are weary and burdened, and I will give you rest. Take my yoke upon you and learn from me, for I am gentle and humble in heart, and you will find rest for your souls. For my yoke is easy and my burden is light."

MATTHEW 11:28–30 NIV

Sometimes life seems like a race that you can never win, and you get tired. Bone weary. You're struggled out.

When life gets you down, there's hope in Jesus. He offers you a deep, soul rest.

The Message paraphrases Matthew 11:28–30 beautifully: "Come to me. Get away with me and you'll recover your life. I'll show you how to take a real rest. Walk with me and work with me—watch how I do it. Learn the unforced rhythms of grace. I won't lay anything heavy or ill-fitting on you. Keep company with me and you'll learn to live freely and lightly."

Your busyness matters to Jesus. Do you want to recover your life? He wants you to come to Him and rest in Him daily, finding a new, unhurried rhythm of grace. As you find this rhythm with Jesus, He fills you with His strength.

LORD, HELP ME LEARN TO LIVE FREELY AND LIGHTLY. I NEED A DEEP SOUL REST. I KNOW THAT SPENDING TIME WITH YOU DAILY IS THE ANSWER.

JESUS IS CLOSE

The eyes of the Lord watch over those who do right; his ears are open to their cries for help. . . . The Lord hears his people when they call to him for help. He rescues them from all their troubles. The Lord is close to the brokenhearted; he rescues those whose spirits are crushed.

Psalm 34:15, 17–18 NLT

Jesus is closer than you think. When your heart is broken, He is with you. When your spirit feels crushed, God is close. God's Word says that He hears your prayers and His eyes are on you. He sees you. You are important to Him, and He loves you more than you could ever imagine. Sit with those truths for a moment. Allow them to wash over you in the midst of your struggles.

Sometimes God will send a person to give you an extra-special dose of love at just the right time. A hug or a message from a friend can lift your head toward God. Sometimes He will supernaturally warm your heart with love as you talk to Him and read His Word. Be on the lookout for His love, and you'll surely find it. He is watching over you and wants to rescue you.

JESUS, OPEN MY EYES TO SEE YOU AT WORK IN MY LIFE. HELP ME KNOW YOU ARE NEAR.

WHEN YOU'RE FEELING LONELY

"For whoever does the will of My Father who is in heaven [by believing in Me, and following Me] is My brother and sister and mother."

MATTHEW 12:50 AMP

Family is important to Jesus. Psalm 68:6 (NIV) tells us that "God sets the lonely in families." He created us to live in community with other believers. We learn from one another and grow and share God's love when we have good relationships with other people.

God doesn't want us to be lonely. Yes, there are times when God uses *feelings* of loneliness to draw us closer to Him. But He doesn't want you to be alone. You are a child of God, so that means you are part of God's family! If you are having a difficult time finding good friends, ask Jesus for help! Ask Him to show you how to get involved in a Jesus-loving, Bible-believing church. If you're seeking Him, He will open the right doors for you. He cares about your relationships and wants you to have the family of God around you to help you in this life.

JESUS, WILL YOU HELP ME FIND OTHER BELIEVERS WHO LOVE YOU AND WANT TO FOLLOW YOU? PLEASE SHOW ME WHAT IT MEANS TO BE A PART OF YOUR FAMILY.

THE STING OF REJECTION

Then Jesus asked them, "Didn't you ever read this in the Scriptures? 'The stone that the builders rejected has now become the cornerstone. This is the LORD's doing, and it is wonderful to see.'"

MATTHEW 21:42 NLT

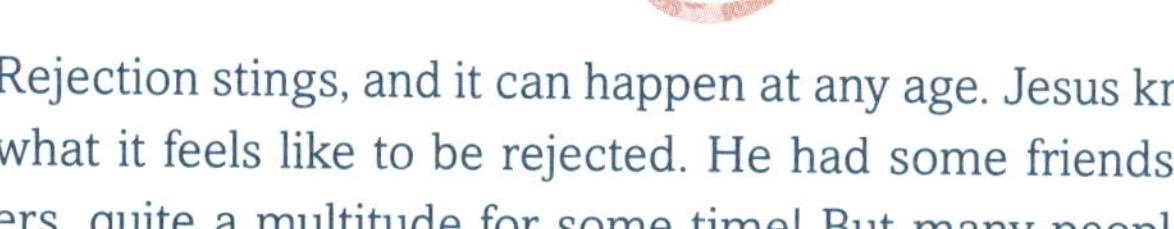

Rejection stings, and it can happen at any age. Jesus knows exactly what it feels like to be rejected. He had some friends and followers, quite a multitude for some time! But many people eventually rejected Him and sent Him to die on a cross. Most of His family didn't believe in Him. Even former friends betrayed Him. The crowds called for Jesus to be crucified. They humiliated Him. He endured all of it out of His deep love for us. People rejected Jesus, but God had chosen Him.

Remember this the next time you feel alone or forgotten. Jesus was perfect in every way, and even He couldn't please everyone. It has been said that you could be the most perfect peach in the bunch, but some people just don't like peaches.

When the sting of rejection hits, remember that God chose you to be His much-loved child. Jesus sees everything that is happening to you, and He understands your heart. He has been where you are. And He is with you right now.

JESUS, THANK YOU FOR ALL THAT YOU ENDURED ON MY BEHALF. YOUR LOVE IS ASTOUNDING.

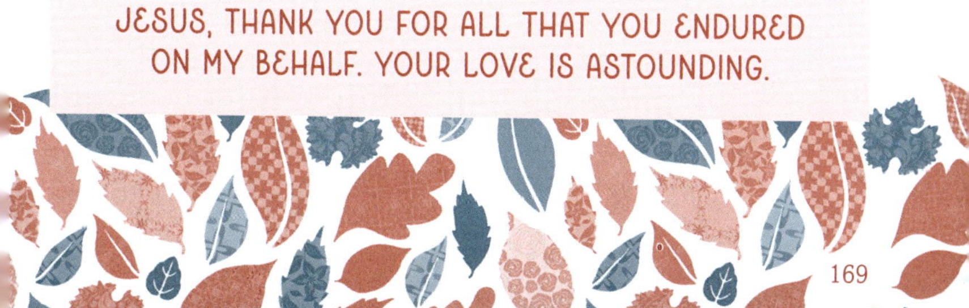

YOUR HELPER AND ADVOCATE

"But the Helper (Comforter, Advocate, Intercessor—Counselor, Strengthener, Standby), the Holy Spirit, whom the Father will send in My name [in My place, to represent Me and act on My behalf], He will teach you all things. And He will help you remember everything that I have told you."

JOHN 14:26 AMP

Look at what Jesus has to say to us in John 16:7 (NIV): "But very truly I tell you, it is for your good that I am going away. Unless I go away, the Advocate will not come to you; but if I go, I will send him to you."

An advocate is a person who comes alongside us and supports us and/or defends us in our time of need. What a divine gift we've been given! The Holy Spirit is our advocate, counselor, teacher, comforter, and guide—the promise that we are never alone fulfilled! The Spirit is the power of God alive inside of everyone who believes and chooses to follow Jesus. Through His power, we have everything we need (2 Peter 1:3). When we don't know what to do, we can ask! When we don't know what to pray, the Spirit helps (Romans 8:26)!

COME, HOLY SPIRIT. FILL MY HEART WITH YOUR PRESENCE AND PEACE. THANK YOU FOR HELPING ME IN EVERYTHING AND IN EVERY WAY.

LAST WORDS

"Teach these new disciples to obey all the commands I have given you. And be sure of this: I am with you always, even to the end of the age."
MATTHEW 28:20 NLT

After Jesus conquered death and rose from the grave, He appeared many times to His followers. The last thing He had to say to them before He went back to heaven is this: "I am with you always."

The last thing someone says to you is usually quite important. Remember that Barbara (her story is on page 78) shared 2 Peter 1:3 (NIV) with our family right before she died: "His divine power has given us everything we need for a godly life through our knowledge of him who called us by his own glory and goodness." That scripture has become a powerful reminder for our family, one we will never forget.

So yes, last words are a big deal. And Matthew 28:20 seems to be the most important thing Jesus wants us to know. He is Immanuel, God with us. Always. His Spirit is alive in our hearts. Any confidence we have is flimsy at best unless it is based on the knowledge that the Spirit of Christ is alive and at work within us!

JESUS, THANK YOU FOR YOUR GREAT LOVE FOR ME. OVERWHELM ME WITH THE TRUTH THAT YOU ARE ALWAYS WITH ME.

HIS GENTLE STRENGTH

Death initially came by a man, and resurrection from death came by a man. Everybody dies in Adam; everybody comes alive in Christ.

1 CORINTHIANS 15:21–22 MSG

Have you ever used your own strength to make a person feel small? Maybe you wanted to win an argument, and your pride came out in full force. Or perhaps you didn't say the words out loud, but you felt superiority in your mind and heart.

Navigating our lives in our own strength can sometimes look and feel like death. Going toe to toe in anger with someone else is often a power struggle due to pride and sin. Confess those things to Jesus. Ask Him to bring to mind any of your relationships that need healing and a heavy dose of humility. Ask Jesus to fill you with His gentle strength. In Matthew 11:29 (NIV), Jesus tells us about Himself: "I am gentle and humble in heart."

As we come alive in Christ, He fills us with the fruit of His Spirit. One of those fruits is gentleness (Galatians 5:22–23). Ask for it in great measure.

JESUS, I CONFESS MY PRIDE TO YOU.
WASH ME IN YOUR GENTLE STRENGTH.

GOD'S POWER IS ON YOUR SIDE

Among the gods there is none like you, Lord; no deeds can compare with yours. All the nations you have made will come and worship before you, Lord; they will bring glory to your name. For you are great and do marvelous deeds; you alone are God.

PSALM 86:8–10 NIV

The time you spend with God will accomplish more than anything else you could ever do. There is no other power greater than our God, and He is on your side! Take a look at these scriptures:

- "Ah, Sovereign LORD, you have made the heavens and the earth by your great power and outstretched arm. Nothing is too hard for you" (Jeremiah 32:17 NIV).
- "Jesus looked at them intently and said, 'Humanly speaking, it is impossible. But with God everything is possible'" (Matthew 19:26 NLT).
- "Now all glory to God, who is able, through his mighty power at work within us, to accomplish infinitely more than we might ask or think" (Ephesians 3:20 NLT).

Ask God to help you believe that He can do anything! No problem is too hard, too big, or too small for God's help.

GOD OF ALL CREATION, THERE IS NO ONE LIKE YOU. I AM SO BLESSED TO BE ABLE TO GIVE EVERYTHING ON MY HEART TO YOU IN PRAYER. I KNOW YOU WANT TO HELP ME!

GOD WILL NEVER LET YOU DOWN

Against all hope, Abraham in hope believed. . . . Yet he did not waver through unbelief regarding the promise of God, but was strengthened in his faith and gave glory to God, being fully persuaded that God had power to do what he had promised.

ROMANS 4:18, 20–21 NIV

If there is one thing you can count on for all eternity, it's that God will never let you down. Romans 4 shares about Abraham's faith in God's promise. *The Message* says, "He didn't tiptoe around God's promise asking cautiously skeptical questions. He plunged into the promise and came up strong, ready for God, sure that God would make good on what he had said."

God always keeps His promises. It may feel like you've been let down because something happened that you don't fully understand, but only God sees all and knows all.

In Revelation 21:6 (NIV), God tells us, "I am the Alpha and the Omega, the Beginning and the End." You can trust His character. You can trust that He is good—all the time.

The heavenly Father doesn't have negative thoughts about you—even when you mess up. Jesus already took all the punishment. God looks on you with love because of Jesus. You can count on it!

YOU ARE GOOD AND FAITHFUL, LORD GOD. I PUT ALL MY TRUST IN YOU!

SKIP AWAY YOUR WORRIES

Let the peace of Christ rule in your hearts, since as members of one body you were called to peace. And be thankful.

COLOSSIANS 3:15 NIV

The Amplified Bible says it this way: "Let the peace of Christ [the inner calm of one who walks daily with Him] be the controlling factor in your hearts [deciding and settling questions that arise]."

Barbara was a dear elderly friend of mine. She would go outside and skip down the road (even in her advanced age) when she was worried about something. She would talk to Jesus as she skipped. She said it made her feel better. When you get in the daily habit of praying and taking all your problems, worries, and concerns to Jesus, you begin to experience the kind of peace He offers.

When you let peace have power over your heart, it means that you have an inner calm that comes from trusting Jesus and walking (or skipping!) with Him daily. When problems come, and they will (remember John 16:33), you trust in Jesus and His power over anything.

When the struggle gets to be too much, turn your focus off yourself and onto Jesus. Skip down the road—and thank God for filling your heart with His peace.

JESUS, HELP ME TO FOCUS ON YOU AND YOUR POWER INSTEAD OF MY PROBLEMS.

A PARENT'S BLESSING

You go before me and follow me. You place your hand of blessing on my head.

PSALM 139:5 NLT

Nothing you could do could make God love you more or less than He does right this very moment. Do you really believe that? Mess-ups and mistakes can't change how much God loves you. Because you are His beloved child, He promises that nothing can separate you from His love (Romans 8:38–39).

Zephaniah 3:17 (NLT) says, "For the LORD your God is living among you. He is a mighty savior. He will take delight in you with gladness. With his love, he will calm all your fears. He will rejoice over you with joyful songs."

God's Word tells us that He goes before us and follows us. His hand of blessing is on us. Does that make you feel secure and fully loved? God is a good dad who always gets it right. He even sings over you!

You may have your own parent wounds that need healing. Maybe you didn't grow up with a parent's blessing. Jesus wants to heal those wounds in your heart. Let Him parent you well, no matter how old you are. We're all in need of a parent's blessing.

LORD, THANK YOU FOR LOVING ME MORE THAN I CAN IMAGINE. PLEASE HEAL MY HEART WOUNDS AND LET ME FEEL YOUR BLESSING.

GOD IS FIGHTING FOR YOU

"God, your God, is leading the way; he's fighting for you. You saw with your own eyes what he did for you in Egypt; you saw what he did in the wilderness, how God, your God, carried you as a father carries his child, carried you the whole way until you arrived here."

DEUTERONOMY 1:30–31 MSG

Any good father, if his beloved child were in danger, would fight to free them from an enemy and carry that child to safety. Our God does this for us too.

Check out these other verses about God fighting for us:

- "The Lord will fight for you; you need only to be still" (Exodus 14:14 NIV).
- "Wherever you hear the sound of the trumpet, join us there. Our God will fight for us!" (Nehemiah 4:20 NIV).
- "'He may have a great army, but they are merely men. We have the Lord our God to help us and to fight our battles for us!' Hezekiah's words greatly encouraged the people" (2 Chronicles 32:8 NLT).
- "This is what the Lord says: Do not be afraid! Don't be discouraged by this mighty army, for the battle is not yours, but God's" (2 Chronicles 20:15 NLT).

Do you need a champion in your life? Trust that God is fighting for you!

THANK YOU FOR BEING A GOOD, GOOD FATHER TO ME!

PEOPLE PROBLEMS

Trust in and rely confidently on the Lord with all your heart and do not rely on your own insight or understanding.

PROVERBS 3:5 AMP

"Hurt people hurt people." Have you heard that saying before? When people act out of control or angry or manipulative, it can be because they are hurting. Maybe they've been treated poorly for most of their lives and don't even realize the way they are acting is wrong. Anger is often just a mask for a deeper emotion. It seems easier to show your anger to someone rather than bare your heart about deep emotional wounds, right?

If you are faced with an angry or hard-to-handle person, do this: Ask the Holy Spirit to give you strength and understanding. Hopefully this will help you have compassion for that difficult person. Pray for them and the problems in their lives as you come into contact with difficult people. They need to know and feel the love of Christ. You may be the first person ever to show them real love. The Holy Spirit can also give you wisdom so that you won't be manipulated in the process.

LORD, HELP ME TO VIEW THE PROBLEM PEOPLE IN MY LIFE AS PEOPLE WHO NEED YOUR UNCONDITIONAL LOVE.

STRENGTH IN TRUTH

"Do not rebel against the Lord, and don't be afraid of the people of the land. They are only helpless prey to us! They have no protection, but the Lord is with us! Don't be afraid of them!"

Numbers 14:9 NLT

Joshua and Caleb, along with several other spies, were sent into the Promised Land to explore and report back to the Israelite people. The other spies gave a bad report that scared the people and caused a rebellion.

Joshua and Caleb faced an angry mob who were ready to stone their leaders. These were people they knew well—their friends and family. Joshua and Caleb were obedient and faithful to God. They pleaded with the people to return to the ways of God. But the people didn't listen, and God gave them dire consequences. God rewarded Joshua and Caleb and allowed them to enter the Promised Land, while everyone else was not permitted.

When God asks you to stand up for Him and His ways among your friends and family, He will give you the courage to speak truth in love (Ephesians 4:15) regardless of the way things turn out. You will be blessed in your obedience even if your words aren't valued by others.

LORD, PLEASE GIVE ME COURAGE TO SPEAK UP FOR YOUR TRUTH EVEN WHEN IT'S DIFFICULT.

STRENGTH WITH PEOPLE

*The Lord is my light and my salvation—
whom shall I fear? The Lord is the stronghold
of my life—of whom shall I be afraid?*

Psalm 27:1 NIV

Do you ever struggle with what other people might think of you? Truth be told, we've probably all had issues with this from time to time. Whatever self-doubt you may be wrestling with, knowing who you are in Christ can make all the difference.

Knowing who you are in Christ gives you supernatural strength and courage that you never had before. Did you know that God chose you? That you are holy and dearly loved? Colossians 3:12 tells us that.

Get into God's Word and uncover the full truth of who you are in Christ. Ask the Holy Spirit to teach you and remind you of who you are. You are a royal daughter of the King of all kings (John 1:12). You are a friend of Christ (John 15:15). You can lift your head because you are God's child (Psalm 3:3). You are seated with Christ in the heavenly realms (Ephesians 2:6–7).

LORD, WHEN I FEEL "LESS THAN" AROUND CERTAIN PEOPLE, REMIND ME THAT I AM YOUR BELOVED CHILD. STRENGTHEN ME TO DO YOUR WILL.

CHOOSE STRENGTH

I [Daniel] said to the one standing in front of me. . . "My strength is gone, and I can hardly breathe." Then the one who looked like a man touched me again, and I felt my strength returning. "Don't be afraid," he said, "for you are very precious to God. Peace! Be encouraged! Be strong!"

DANIEL 10:16–19 NLT

Has your household ever passed the flu around? The sickness that never seems to go away, with the cough that lingers on and on? It's easy to get to the point of not caring about much of anything when you feel that bad. You just want to sleep through it and feel better. So, you'll do anything you can to feel better fast. Whatever pill will work. Whatever food sounds good. Whatever shows you can binge to bring some relief.

Don't avoid God when you feel like this. Tell Him how you feel. Be real about it. Let these scriptures in Daniel encourage you: "Lord, I feel terrible. I don't want to think or feel. Please help me!"

God is the same yesterday, today, and forever. You are very precious to Him. Choose to be strengthened by Him instead of giving in to the temptation to binge on temporary relief for days on end.

LORD, I ASK YOU TO STRENGTHEN ME JUST AS YOU STRENGTHENED DANIEL. I CHOOSE YOU TODAY, TOMORROW, AND ALL OF MY DAYS TO COME.

THE LORD, MY STRENGTH

I love you, God—you make me strong. God is bedrock under my feet, the castle in which I live, my rescuing knight. My God—the high crag where I run for dear life, hiding behind the boulders, safe in the granite hideout.

Psalm 18:1–2 MSG

God arms us with strength. Psalm 18:32 (NIV) tells us that. Take a look: "It is God who arms me with strength and keeps my way secure." What does it mean to be "armed"? One way to define it is "supplied with equipment, tools, or other items in preparation or readiness for something."

So, if you're armed with strength from God, you are supplied with everything you need from God Himself. You are prepared and ready for anything that comes your way.

The Bible uses a lot of imagery to connect us more fully with God. Can you picture Jesus arming you with His strength and power? Do you trust Him to keep you secure? Invite God to speak to you about this. Write down anything He impresses upon your heart and any other scripture the Holy Spirit brings to mind. Journaling is a spiritual practice intended to help you remember all that God is teaching you in your journey.

THANK YOU, LORD, FOR ARMING ME WITH YOUR STRENGTH. I KNOW IT COMES FROM YOU ALONE.

BROAD SHOULDERS

Pile your troubles on GOD*'s shoulders—he'll carry your load, he'll help you out. He'll never let good people topple into ruin.*

PSALM 55:22 MSG

Have you ever felt the weight of the world on your shoulders? The burdens women try to carry on their shoulders can cause so many problems. If you're feeling weighed down, it's time to surrender those burdens to Jesus. His shoulders are broad and meant to carry your load. Cast your cares, worries, and anxiety on Him (1 Peter 5:7).

Psalm 81:6–7 (MSG) says, "I took the world off your shoulders, freed you from a life of hard labor. You called to me in your pain; I got you out of a bad place."

You may be in a situation where you have a lot of decisions to make that affect other people. Maybe you're the boss at the office. Maybe other people are counting on you to help them through a difficult situation. Whatever is weighing on you, hear this: It's not all up to you. *Read that again.*

God has plans and purposes for you and for every person you are concerned about. He is there to help you make decisions. He has plans you may know nothing about for that person. You can trust Him.

I'M SHIFTING MY BURDENS TO YOUR SHOULDERS, LORD. I TRUST YOU TO TAKE THEM ALL!

SEEING THE FRUIT

But don't just listen to God's word. You must do what it says. Otherwise, you are only fooling yourselves.

JAMES 1:22 NLT

If you've made it this far and you agree with every devotion that has been written to this point, great! Now what do you intend to do about it? *The Message* cautions not to let "the Word go in one ear and out the other."

If you want to see the fruit of finding strength in the struggles, you have to let God's Word take root in your heart and come out through your actions.

A friend of mine was struggling with a relationship that involved one of her children and their family. She was worried and didn't know what to do. She had done everything she could to make the situation right on her end. But she was still worried, and it was making her physically ill. She cried out to God, asking for His mercy and grace to cover the situation and the people involved. She took her thoughts captive and surrendered the situation to Jesus before going to bed.

The next morning, beautiful resolution came to light! She had trusted God and surrendered, and He resolved the situation perfectly—as only He can.

GOD, I BELIEVE THAT YOUR WORD IS REAL AND TRUE AND HAS POWER TODAY! HELP ME TO TAKE YOU AT YOUR WORD AND ACTIVELY TRUST YOU.

THE SPIRIT PRAYS FOR US

Meanwhile, the moment we get tired in the waiting, God's Spirit is right alongside helping us along. If we don't know how or what to pray, it doesn't matter. He does our praying in and for us, making prayer out of our wordless sighs, our aching groans. He knows us far better than we know ourselves. . .and keeps us present before God.

ROMANS 8:26–27 MSG

There are days when you don't feel like praying. Or you get distracted and start scrolling on social media before you start praying. You're not alone. Jesus is very aware of the human condition because He became one of us. God knows how you feel and why. That's why He has sent His Spirit to live inside of us. To encourage us always—and to convict and counsel us. He is our "Helper (Comforter, Advocate, Intercessor—Counselor, Strengthener, Standby)" (John 14:26 AMP).

The Spirit of God will pray in us and for us when we don't know what to pray for or when we just don't feel like it. If you are feeling this way today, sit quietly somewhere and just breathe. Ask the Holy Spirit to pray for you. Remove the distractions. Ask Him to convict your heart to do His will.

FATHER, I THANK YOU FOR SENDING YOUR SPIRIT TO PRAY FOR ME. YOU KNOW MY HEART AND EVERYTHING I NEED.

THE POWER OF PRAYER

Therefore, confess your sins to one another [your false steps, your offenses], and pray for one another, that you may be healed and restored. The heartfelt and persistent prayer of a righteous man (believer) can accomplish much [when put into action and made effective by God—it is dynamic and can have tremendous power].

JAMES 5:16 AMP

Prayer is powerful. Not only do we get to know God better when we talk to Him, but our prayers can make things happen.

Ephesians 6:19–20 (NIV) says, "Pray also for me, that whenever I speak, words may be given me so that I will fearlessly make known the mystery of the gospel, for which I am an ambassador in chains. Pray that I may declare it fearlessly, as I should."

What happens when we pray has some mystery to it! But we know that God hears us (1 Peter 3:12). God's Word tells us to pray for others so that they can be healed and restored. This means not only that physical bodies can be healed but that broken hearts can be mended.

Bring whatever is on your heart today to Jesus for healing. Which friends and family members need His loving touch? Your prayers can make all the difference!

LORD, THANK YOU FOR HEARING MY PRAYERS.
REMIND ME AGAIN HOW POWERFUL IT IS TO PRAY.

A LIFE OF PRAYER

Very early in the morning, while it was still dark, Jesus got up, left the house and went off to a solitary place, where he prayed.

MARK 1:35 NIV

The Bible says that Jesus often went away to be alone with God and pray. Jesus was fully God and fully human. And He knew where His power came from. He submitted Himself to His heavenly Father and showed us how to do the same. As a follower of Jesus, you have power and hope and strength to make it through each day that come from your time spent with God.

Jesus lived a life of prayer. He did nothing outside the will of His Father—your Father! Because of Jesus and all that He accomplished through His death and resurrection, you have complete access to our heavenly Father too.

How can you live a life of prayer like Jesus did? You invite Him into every moment of your day. You seek His thoughts when you need help, fixing your eyes on Him (Hebrews 12:2). You ask Him to give you love for others as you interact with the people you come across. You submit yourself to His will.

LORD, I WANT TO OBEY YOU BECAUSE
I LOVE YOU. I SUBMIT MYSELF TO YOU.
SHOW ME HOW TO LIVE A LIFE OF PRAYER.

BEGIN AND END WITH JESUS

[Not in your own strength] for it is God Who is all the while effectually at work in you [energizing and creating in you the power and desire], both to will and to work for His good pleasure and satisfaction and delight.

PHILIPPIANS 2:13 AMPC

What have we learned in our time together, friend? Hopefully you're starting to understand that the strength to live the Christian life comes from Jesus Christ Himself. He is the one who gives the energy to do what He has called you to do. He is the one creating the power and the desire to follow His will. You never have to dig deep and muster that strength yourself. That's the opposite of what God wants for you.

One day the struggles we face will end. Revelation 21:4 (NIV) promises us that "'He will wipe every tear from their eyes. There will be no more death' or mourning or crying or pain, for the old order of things has passed away." But until then, remember that you are not alone in your struggle. You have Holy Spirit power alive and at work in you, comforting you in life's heartaches and struggles and strengthening you as you spend time in His presence.

LORD GOD, I'M SO THANKFUL FOR WHAT YOU'RE TEACHING ME ABOUT YOUR STRENGTH AT WORK IN ME.

SCRIPTURE INDEX